364.1523 LAM
Lamb, America.
Deadly dose : the untold
story of a homicide in
9780425221969 KR1

AUG 2008

DEADLY DOSE

D1618409

Most Berkley Books are available at special quantity discounts for bulk purchases for sales promotions, premiums, fund-raising, or educational use. Special books, or book excerpts, can also be created to fit specific needs.

For details, write: Special Markets, The Berkley Publishing Group, 375 Hudson Street, New York, New York 10014.

DEADLY DOSE

The Untold Story of a Homicide Investigator's Crusade
for Truth and Justice

Amanda Lamb

BERKLEY BOOKS, NEW YORK

THE BERKLEY PUBLISHING GROUP
Published by the Penguin Group
Penguin Group (USA) Inc.
375 Hudson Street, New York, New York 10014, USA
Penguin Group (Canada), 90 Eglinton Avenue East, Suite 700, Toronto, Ontario M4P 2Y3, Canada
(a division of Pearson Penguin Canada Inc.)
Penguin Books Ltd., 80 Strand, London WC2R 0RL, England
Penguin Group Ireland, 25 St. Stephen's Green, Dublin 2, Ireland (a division of Penguin Books Ltd.)
Penguin Group (Australia), 250 Camberwell Road, Camberwell, Victoria 3124, Australia
(a division of Pearson Australia Group Pty. Ltd.)
Penguin Books India Pvt. Ltd., 11 Community Centre, Panchsheel Park, New Delhi—110 017, India
Penguin Group (NZ), 67 Apollo Drive, Rosedale, North Shore 0632, New Zealand
(a division of Pearson New Zealand Ltd.)
Penguin Books (South Africa) (Pty.) Ltd., 24 Sturdee Avenue, Rosebank, Johannesburg 2196,
South Africa

Penguin Books Ltd., Registered Offices: 80 Strand, London WC2R 0RL, England

DEADLY DOSE

A Berkley Book / published by arrangement with the author

PRINTING HISTORY
Berkley mass-market edition / June 2008

Copyright © 2008 by Amanda Lamb
Cover design by Diana Kolsky
Cover photograph: "Raleigh City Lights at Dusk" © Joseph Sohm/Visions of America/Corbis
Book design by Kristin del Rosario

All rights reserved.
No part of this book may be reproduced, scanned, or distributed in any printed or electronic form
without permission. Please do not participate in or encourage piracy of copyrighted materials in
violation of the author's rights. Purchase only authorized editions.
For information, address: The Berkley Publishing Group,
a division of Penguin Group (USA) Inc.,
375 Hudson Street, New York, New York 10014.

ISBN: 978-0-425-22196-9

BERKLEY®
Berkley Books are published by The Berkley Publishing Group,
a division of Penguin Group (USA) Inc.,
375 Hudson Street, New York, New York 10014.
BERKLEY is a registered trademark of Penguin Group (USA) Inc.
The "B" design is a trademark belonging to Penguin Group (USA) Inc.

PRINTED IN THE UNITED STATES OF AMERICA

10 9 8 7 6 5 4 3 2 1

If you purchased this book without a cover, you should be aware that this book is stolen property. It was
reported as "unsold and destroyed" to the publisher, and neither the author nor the publisher has
received any payment for this "stripped book."

PROLOGUE

We all live under the same sky,
but we don't all have the same horizon.
—KONRAD ADENAUER

Investigator Chris Morgan leans back slowly into the crevices of his worn leather recliner like he's sinking into a hot bath. The dark brown material is stretched and broken from years of abuse, like a snake skin left by the side of the road in the scorching sunlight. The chair sticks to his large bare arms and surrounds him like an old familiar blanket. Over the years, his wife has begged him to get rid of the ugly old chair. But no other chair fits his ample frame quite like this one. It is here, in his chair, in the darkness of his study, in his room, that he tells the story that almost consumed the latter part of his life.

For Morgan there are two kinds of murderers. There is the impersonal murderer who kills for money. Often, the victim dies quickly and suffers little at the hands of this killer. But then there are murderers who revel in watching people die. They get joy and power from seeing their

1

victims suffer. Ann Miller watched her husband, Dr. Eric Miller, die a thousand small deaths over a period of months before his heart finally stopped at 2:50 a.m. on Saturday, December 2, 2000, at Rex Hospital in Raleigh, North Carolina.

To die from chronic arsenic poisoning is to be slowly tortured. Morgan has read everything he can find on the subject. He learned how arsenic attacks all of the tissues in your body and severely limits your ability to function. The first symptoms are flulike—nausea, vomiting, and diarrhea. Early on, the damage can be reversed if the exposure stops. But if it continues, the toxic chemical attacks your nerves, your stomach, your intestines, and your skin. You feel excruciating pain and eventually become psychotic. It is as if your body is slowly deteriorating, being eaten away, and one day, one painful day, it finally gives out for good.

North Carolina is no stranger to high-profile arsenic poisonings. Most often, the details are the stuff made-for-television movies are fashioned from. Forty-six-year-old Velma Barfield did it to her lover, Stuart Taylor, just before they dressed up in their Sunday best and went to see a visiting evangelist at the local convention center. Investigators soon learned many people close to Barfield had died under "suspicious circumstances." She was ultimately convicted of killing Taylor and put to death in 1984.

Blanche Taylor Moore sits in a North Carolina prison condemned to death after being convicted of poisoning her boyfriend, Raymond Reid, with arsenic in 1986. In addition to Reid, investigators determined that Moore's first and second husbands were also poisoned with arsenic. Her first husband died, yet Moore was charged only in Reid's case. But it took only one case to put her on death row.

As many times as he has gone over it in his mind, Morgan can't comprehend why a promising thirty-year-old pediatric AIDS researcher had to die this way. Eric Miller was the kind of man no one disliked. Morgan never knew him when he was alive, but after hundreds of interviews with people who did know Eric, Morgan now counts him as a friend.

Morgan readjusts his formidable frame and eases a little bit deeper into the comfortable chair, so deep he fears it might collapse beneath his ample weight. The house is quiet without his four children living at home. In the distance his dog barks manically from the yard. Morgan hears his wife, Kay, scolding, trying to usher the pet back inside. He takes another pinch of chewing tobacco. His story will take time to tell. It cascades out of his mouth in long, deliberate run-on sentences, like a poet searching for the right cadence.

Ann Miller was an attractive woman, a well-educated scientist, a mother, an active church member. Not the kind of woman anyone would've suspected of killing her husband; no one except perhaps Chris Morgan. Yet over the five-year period following Eric Miller's death, Ann Miller left a string of lies, and a history of manipulation, hypocrisy, and more death in her path. Despite her prim and proper appearance, Ann Miller was serially unfaithful to her husband. Morgan always felt she had an uncanny power not only to lure men into her web of seduction, but to then cast them aside when she no longer needed what they had to offer.

For years Ann Miller remained free and seemingly unflustered by the deaths she left in her wake. During this time Morgan refused to give up the fight to put her behind bars. As a leader of the Major Crimes Task Force, he was on her heels day and night. From the beginning he suspected that Ann Miller was the killer. He pressured the district attorney almost daily to take the case to court.

Crusader is not a word to be used lightly. But in this case it fits. Chris Morgan is a crusader in every sense of the word.

This is his story, as told from an old recliner in a small, comfortable ranch house somewhere in rural North Carolina. It is getting dark now as the late-winter sun sets in the distance, sending only a small shaft of light across his weathered face. He has traveled many miles to get to this day. He is ready.

ONE

Fate determines many things
no matter how we struggle.
—OTTO WEININGER

The longer you live, the more you realize that while first impressions may not *always* be right, they *usually* are.

From the moment Investigator Chris Morgan saw thirty-year-old Ann Miller through the window of the interview room at the Raleigh Police Department on December 2, 2000, he knew something was wrong. Her image from that night is etched into his mind with the crystal-clear clarity of a black-and-white photograph. It has a timeless quality about it that never fades, never gets grainy, never curls or turns yellow around the edges. Indeed, it became only sharper as the years went by.

"I got that funny little feeling in the back of my mind," Morgan says, recalling his peek at Ann through the interview-room window that cold winter night. It was a feeling that had served Morgan well in his twenty-nine years as a cop. He spent most of the last decade investigating

5

murders, but this case stayed with him like a bad rash that wouldn't go away.

Ann Miller, a scientist at the then-named pharmaceutical giant Glaxo Wellcome, was wrapped in an afghan and huddled against her father in a small waiting room. She was waiting to be interviewed by investigators about the death of her husband, Eric Miller. Thirty-year-old Dr. Eric Miller, a pediatric AIDS researcher at the Lineberger Comprehensive Cancer Center at UNC Hospitals, had died at Rex Hospital in Raleigh, North Carolina, at 2:50 a.m. that morning. The cause—*arsenic poisoning*. He took his last breath never knowing what hit him.

Eric was a tall, thin, handsome man, with a head full of thick brown hair and a smile for every camera lens. Morgan still looks at Eric's pictures often, and is surprisingly comforted by them. They show a man full of life, full of promise, a man who was not supposed to die young. A man Morgan would have liked to have known.

Morgan himself is a large, imposing man with sprigs of white hair and a worn face that reveals the time he spent in the trenches as a homicide investigator. He walks slowly, and speaks slowly, letting each thought roll off his tongue with a combination of southern redneck and unlikely academic thrown in. He usually wears a white fedora, and beneath the brim, if he tips his hat, you might catch a glimpse of twinkling blue eyes indicating a man full of curiosity.

"Something just wasn't ringing true," says Morgan of that night when he first saw Ann Miller. Ann was not a tiny woman—at five feet five inches and 140 pounds, she was average by most standards—but there was something about her highlighted mousy-brown shoulder-length hair, her soft blue eyes, and the way she leaned in to her father for comfort that made her look more diminutive and frail than she really was. In Morgan's estimation, the helpless-little-girl look was part of her power, her control over others. It made people want to take care of her. And it worked.

"The more I thought, the more I flashed back to seeing her sitting there looking the way she did. Like I say, she was prim, proper. The more I thought this isn't an accident, this isn't any suicide. This is a *murder*."

STUMBLING INTO THE CASE

In 2000, Morgan was a sergeant heading up one of two squads of the Major Crimes Task Force for the Raleigh Police Department. On the weekend of December 2, 2000, he wasn't scheduled to work, but instead was preparing to head to the western part of the state for a homicide conference to present information he had collected in a 1994 cold case of a young murder victim named Beth-Ellen Vinson.

Morgan had been asked to reinvestigate the unsolved murder by police chief Mitch Brown. For a year, Morgan had poured his heart and soul into reworking the cold case. Not unlike every other case he doggedly pursued, Morgan took an emotional and intensely personal interest in Beth-Ellen and her family. He had brought his findings, complete with a detailed PowerPoint presentation, to Wake County district attorney Colon Willoughby. But Willoughby felt he still needed more evidence to get a conviction in a courtroom. Dejected after putting so much effort into what he thought was a solid case, Morgan hoped his colleagues at the conference could help him come up with a different approach to pitch the case again to district attorneys. Still, this disappointment clouded his opinion of the Wake County District Attorney's Office and would set the tone for his future dealings with local prosecutors.

On the night of December 2, 2000, Morgan had stopped by the police station to pick up some paperwork for his presentation at the conference. He was optimistic that his colleagues at the meeting could help him come up with a new way to sell his theories to Willoughby, given the opportunity. But as it turned out, Morgan never made it to the conference. Instead, he became deeply embroiled in the murder of Eric Miller.

When Morgan walked down the hallway in the Major Crimes Division that night, he sensed a familiar energy. Something was going on. There was a buzz in the air, in the hushed tones, in the way his heart started beating faster. The buzz invigorated him. He wanted to know, *needed* to know, what was going on. His gut told him that it was not his shift, not his squad, not his problem. But he couldn't resist. The gravitational pull of a new crime to solve was like a drug to Morgan. No matter how hard he tried to conquer the addiction, he kept coming back for more. And the more he had, the more he wanted. It was a vicious cycle that lasted until the day he retired, and many would say even beyond that.

He asked some questions and the other cops told him a

scientist named Eric Miller had died of arsenic poisoning earlier that morning at Rex Hospital.

Initially, investigators cast a wide net looking for arsenic sources. They told Morgan they were looking at everything from environmental causes to suicide. Morgan wondered out loud how someone would get exposed to arsenic accidentally, since laws required strict guidelines in water systems and food sources in order to prevent contamination from toxic chemicals like arsenic. But after all, Miller *had* been a scientist, working in a laboratory where chemicals were present. Perhaps he'd been accidentally exposed to arsenic in his own lab. Considering how very rare arsenic poisoning is, it seemed like a plausible explanation.

Although suicide, as difficult as it can be to talk about, is one of the first things investigators must rule out in the early stages of a death investigation, detectives working on the case told Morgan that nothing in Eric Miller's background or profile even mildly suggested any kind of emotional problems or depression that might lead to him taking his life.

Morgan sensed that investigators were reluctant to explore the next possibility after accident or suicide—murder. Maybe no one could believe that anyone would want to kill an all-around nice guy like Eric Miller. Maybe they just didn't want to believe that his equally well-educated, attractive wife could have had anything to do with her husband's death.

As Morgan listened to more about the case, his gut kept trying to tell him something. He kept going back to the image of Ann Miller he'd glimpsed just a few minutes earlier through the window of the interview room. Right then and there he had formed an opinion about Ann Miller: she had something to do with her husband's death. It was an opinion that would stick with him, unwavering in its intensity. It was an opinion that would drive him to pursue this case relentlessly until Eric Miller's killer was behind bars.

Morgan was flabbergasted when detectives told him that Ann Miller had come to the police station that night with her father in tow. He was still more flabbergasted when he learned that the sergeant in charge of the investigation had agreed to let Ann Miller's father, Dan Brier, into the interview room with her because it was the only way she would agree to answer their questions. Certainly, the police would be at a disadvantage in this situation. The woman was obviously not going to come clean with her daddy by her side, and the police wouldn't be able to really break her down and get to the truth as long as he was there to protect her. As Morgan saw it, the sergeant felt he'd had no choice if he wanted to talk to the dead man's wife at all. But still, Morgan felt strongly that having her father there had tremendously chilled Ann Miller's statement.

"I said: 'With her *daddy*?'" Morgan recalls. Who knows how differently things might have gone if detectives had been able to talk to Ann Miller by herself?

THE INTERVIEW

Detectives Randy Miller (no relation to Ann or Eric) and Debbie Regentin conducted that first interview with Ann Miller as her father sat hip to hip by her, monitoring every word. Ann told detectives that the entire family, including their almost-one-year-old daughter, Clare, had been sick with flulike symptoms, but that Eric had been hit the hardest.

"The day Clare got sick," Ann said in the official police transcript of the interview, "we went to lunch in a restaurant. I don't know where it was. I remember it was [called] Barry's Café. Eric was giving her French fries because she liked them. She loved them and he had given them to her and she threw up. I got mad at him for giving her French fries. I told him her little tummy could not handle the grease yet," she said as tears rolled down her pale face.

"It's okay," said Detective Regentin.

"I would let him feed her French fries every day if I could have him back," Ann said, sobbing.

"I know," Regentin said.

"I miss him so bad," said Ann.

Detectives working on the case told Morgan that they had no reason initially to believe Ann Miller had anything to do with her husband's death. They wanted to give her time to grieve, recalls Morgan, and decided to reinterview her after the funeral a few days later.

But Raleigh police never got another chance to talk to Ann Miller. Shortly after that first night in the police station, unbeknownst to investigators, Ann retained one of the top attorneys in North Carolina, Wade Smith. Smith had gained a national reputation after representing Dr. Jeffrey MacDonald, the Fort Bragg Green Beret convicted of killing his entire family. Years later, Wade Smith would go on to represent a member of the Duke lacrosse team charged with raping an exotic dancer—a client who was later exonerated, many believed, in large part because of Smith's expertise. Smith was also the attorney for the family of Cho Seung Hui, the Virginia Tech shooter who killed thirty-two people as well as himself. Smith was the quintessential southern gentleman, professional and charming in the courtroom despite the often unsavory charges his clients faced. Having him on your side was like having a monumental life insurance policy; it cost a lot, but it practically guaranteed that you would be covered no matter what came your way.

After Ann Miller's initial interview with police, Wade Smith wisely shut the police out from further contact with his client.

"Usually, innocent people don't need to go out and lay down the kind of money that it requires to retain the likes of Mr. Wade Smith," says Morgan.

For Morgan, this was just another red flag in what would become a long series of red flags that made him pause and think about who Ann Miller really was. Morgan is a straight shooter. He knows criminals. He knows what they do, and what they don't do. He also knows how innocent people act and how they don't act. Most importantly, he knows the difference.

On that first night, no one asked Ann Miller the magic question: *Did you kill your husband?* The transcript doesn't lie. According to Morgan, no one asked the direct question because the detectives did not yet consider her a suspect. They did not go where Morgan says every investigation needs to go—directly into the inner circle of someone's life. This was, and still is, one of the aspects of the case Morgan just cannot shake. In Morgan's opinion, not asking this question violated the most basic tenet of murder investigations. You always start close to the victim and then work your way out. He calls this a "universal truth" of homicide investigations. People's lives are like a series of concentric circles. Most people are killed by someone close to them. Women are almost always killed by a husband or a boyfriend. When women kill, the victims are typically husbands, boyfriends, or children. Logically, investigators usually rule out family members and other people who have intimate relationships with the victim first before they look elsewhere for the killer. Rarely do you ever get to a far-reaching circle where a stranger or serial murderer lurks. Good investigators start at home, and then move on to the workplace, friends, and acquaintances.

Morgan claims that if he were murdered, he would expect the same protocol to be used in trying to find his killer.

"Whoever the investigator is, you're *damn* right I want him looking at my wife, looking at my family, my children, even my brother," he says, not hiding the anger as he strains his vocal cords and readjusts his large frame in his squeaky chair.

When it came to murder Morgan never worried about offending people or hurting their feelings. When he was in charge of a case, he always asked the tough questions. If the people he was interviewing were innocent, they would understand why you had to ask; if they were guilty, they would most likely become indignant. *Bingo,* you have your answer.

But for reasons Morgan cannot seem to pinpoint to this day, he felt his colleagues were looking away from Ann Miller instead of at her. It was not his case, it did not happen on his watch, but he could not shake the feeling that this woman might be about to get away with murder if he didn't do something. He tried to stay out of it. But just like everything else Chris Morgan ever tried to stay out of, he seemed to stumble right into the middle of it.

"We know Ann Miller didn't waste any time," says Morgan. But, "I'm afraid *we* did."

INVESTIGATION UNDER WAY

Morgan and the head of the squad handling the Eric Miller case, Sergeant Jeff Fluck, had always had different philosophies about police work. Morgan tended to move faster, with more bravado, taking more risks. Morgan describes Sergeant Fluck as more calculated. He was someone who dotted his *i*'s and crossed his *t*'s, who colored inside the lines, while Morgan was frenetically scribbling all over the page.

Morgan sees an equal need for these two very different styles of policing, though, and respected Sergeant Fluck for his thoroughness and attention to detail. In that first week of the investigation, Fluck's team had begun immediately searching computers. They scoured Eric and Ann's work and home computers for anything that might help them solve the case. While computer forensics takes time; documents the author thought had vanished into the black hole of cyberspace can be retrieved. Hence the famous adage about not writing anything down you don't want someone to read applies to computers maybe even more than it does to paper and pen.

Finally, there was a carrot dangled in front of Morgan. Sergeant Fluck asked Morgan's squad to interview doctors and nurses at Rex Hospital, where Eric Miller died. Morgan was eager to get involved in the case in any way he could, and he would soon find out that Eric Miller's death at the hospital was neither where the case began nor where it would end.

MEDICAL MINDS

While Eric Miller's preliminary autopsy report did not show high levels of arsenic in his body at the time of his death, he'd been hospitalized earlier, in mid-November, and some of those test results from Rex Hospital were showing massive amounts of arsenic in him at that time. Everyone Morgan consulted with told him that the levels were simply too high to have been the result of an accidental or environmental exposure.

Experts also told Morgan that arsenic stays in the bloodstream for only a short period of time and then dissipates if the person is not exposed again in a short time frame. But more detailed tests, using hair samples, can reveal intermittent exposure to arsenic over a prolonged period of time.

Morgan says the staff at the hospital was cooperative

and genuinely broken up about Eric's death. "They were sorry this happened and they didn't know what to make of it," says Morgan. He was not going after them; quite the opposite. Morgan recalls that the attending physician, Dr. Mehna Mohan, seemed sincerely sad about Eric's passing. He remembers Mohan as very emotional at the mere mention of Eric's death. Unlike most doctors he knew, who preferred professional detachment, Mohan was not afraid to cry real tears when she talked about Eric and how he had suffered before he died.

Morgan suspected that no one at the hospital had ever had any experience with arsenic poisoning before. Why should they? Morgan himself had never personally come across an arsenic death in his quarter century of police work. Given the rarity, it was no surprise that arsenic was not immediately suspected by doctors as the cause of Eric Miller's illness.

It was also no surprise that each interview included hospital attorneys, considering the litigious nature of the world today and how it has adversely affected medical institutions. The presence of the attorneys neither intimidated Morgan nor hindered his efforts. He was not someone easily ruffled by men in suits with bigger paychecks than he could ever dream of earning. But the lawyers let him do his job, and he let them do theirs.

"I guess they had already gotten the feeling there was a little bit of blood in the water; turned out they were right," Morgan says caustically.

THE TRAIL

Morgan learned that Ann Miller first took Eric to Rex Hospital on the night of Thursday, November 16, 2000. Although Eric had been to the doctor's office for minor symptoms over the past few months, this was his first visit to the hospital. On this night he complained of severe stomach pains following a bowling outing with a group of Ann's colleagues the previous evening. Investigators learned that he then spent hours in the emergency room waiting to be seen, and it wasn't until the early-morning hours of Friday, November 17, that he was finally admitted to a private room.

Doctors and nurses told Morgan that Eric's condition continued to worsen after he was admitted. Given this turn of events, they made the decision to transfer him to the intensive care unit the next morning.

At 10 a.m. on Saturday, November 18, just two hours after Eric was sent to the ICU, Morgan says Ann decided to get her hair done. The appointment had originally been scheduled for Eric, but instead of sitting by her husband's bedside, Ann decided to appropriate the appointment for herself.

"It was just very bizarre, almost, that Ann had gone in not to get a quick shampoo, maybe a little trim, but [that] she went in and told this hairdresser that she wanted to experiment with a new look," Morgan says, shaking his head along with his words. "There's something wrong with that. There would be something wrong with it if my wife did it. It's not what would be expected of a normal spouse in this situation, male or female. It's just not what people would do."

It reminds Morgan, as this case would so many times later, of the Laci Peterson case. In December 2002, the eight-months pregnant California woman disappeared, and months later her body and the body of her unborn child, Conner, were found along the shores of San Francisco Bay. When investigators checked her husband's computer, they learned that while Laci was missing, Scott Peterson (later convicted of his wife's murder) had spent the time casually surfing the Internet rather than searching for her.

On the evening of November 18, the day Eric was moved to the ICU, Morgan says Dr. William Berry, a Rex Hospital cardiologist, began to suspect arsenic poisoning as a potential cause of Eric's bizarre, undiagnosed symptoms.

Morgan was especially impressed with Dr. Berry for being the first person to go out on a limb and suspect something unconventional. Instead of simply labeling Eric's symptoms the result of some kind of rare virus, Dr. Berry went back to his basic medical training and began looking for outside factors that could cause such symptoms.

On November 19, Dr. Berry ordered a heavy-metals test be performed on Eric Miller to see if his suspicion was accurate. The next day a preliminary test came back showing that Eric had .93 milligrams of arsenic in his blood—a "huge amount," Morgan says.

Because his condition was continuing to deteriorate, on November 21, Eric was transferred from Rex Hospital to a medical facility with more resources, the University of North Carolina Hospitals in Chapel Hill. Morgan explains that the staff at Rex felt Eric needed higher-level care than they could offer him.

On November 22, Dr. Mehna Mohan, one of Eric Miller's doctors at Rex hospital, called Dr. Paul Lawrence Wang, a third-year resident who had taken over Eric's care at UNC. Morgan says Mohan wanted to fill Wang in on the results of the arsenic test taken on November 19. This, Morgan feels, is where a critical miscommunication occurred.

"Dr. Mohan is giving, or quoting, lab results to the doctors at Chapel Hill and what she is giving them is a blood level, but they hear it as a urine level and therein lies the problem," says Morgan, shaking his head. "The reading she was giving him for a blood level was astronomical and toxic, deadly toxic. The readings, if you interpreted them as a urine level, were maybe toxic, but not anything fatal."

Yet Morgan says his concerns about which tests were performed, how quickly they came back, and what was communicated to UNC Hospitals had nothing to do with the criminal investigation. He wasn't a doctor, nor were his detectives. They didn't have the medical background to judge what the doctors had or had not done. Could Eric's death have been prevented if the arsenic had been zeroed in on earlier? Probably, Morgan thinks. But in Morgan's estimation, the men and women who tried to save Eric Miller's life were not responsible for his death.

In his heart Morgan believed a single person was responsible for Eric Miller's murder. It became his mission to find out who had administered the deadly dose of arsenic that ultimately claimed the young scientist's life.

LAB MATES

The case really began to unfold when investigators started talking to people who worked with Ann and Eric. It was not necessarily what these interviewees said; it was more often what they did *not* say that aroused suspicions. A single thread leading from Ann to her husband's death began to form. It took many twists and turns along the way; so many, Morgan probably would have turned around in the very beginning if he'd known what was coming down the road.

Morgan specifically remembers one interview with a coworker of Ann's at Glaxo Wellcome named Liping Wang (no relation to Dr. Wang). Wang shared a cubicle with Ann and was also friends with Eric. She had once worked in Eric's lab at UNC Hospitals, and subsequently, Eric had recommended her for a job with Ann's pharmaceutical company.

"That first interview with [Liping Wang] was kind of strange," Morgan says, a chuckle punctuating the end of his sentence. "Number one, it was one of the few interviews I had ever done with my shoes off."

Morgan remembers how he and Detective Don Terry arrived at Wang's home one evening and saw shoes lined up by the door. Morgan assumed the lush, clean, white carpet in the hallway was the reason for the shoeless protocol and directed Terry to follow his lead and remove his shoes as well. Morgan felt slightly silly sitting at Wang's dining-room table in his three-piece suit, his fedora, and his socks. But as an investigator, he'd always had a "when in Rome" attitude. It was critical in order to gain someone's trust and confidence. You had to earn it. You had to prove you could adapt to their rules when you were on their turf.

Wang served the detectives green tea in dainty china cups. Again, this was no coffee-and-donuts meeting in a Crown Victoria like most cops were used to, but they accepted Wang's hospitality graciously. Morgan admits he actually kind of enjoyed the tea. Yet, given the nature of the investigation—*poisoning*—Terry was not thrilled at the idea of drinking unknown tea offered by a stranger.

Like any experienced investigator, Morgan asked the same questions over and over again, hoping to get to the truth of how Wang perceived Ann's relationship with her husband. But over and over again, he says Wang gave them the same story, using slightly different words. She gushed about what a good marriage Ann and Eric had, about how they were perfectly suited for each other. Morgan feels that it may have been a story Wang had been telling herself repeatedly because the alternative was too difficult to comprehend.

" 'What a happy couple they were!' " Morgan says, mimicking Wang's tone with fake exuberance. "Before it was over with, I said, 'Something is not right here.' "

SIDELINED

Morgan always trusted his gut, and his gut was telling him there was a lot more to this story than anyone truly understood, including him. But again, it was not his case. It was

Jeff Fluck's case. Morgan's access to information was limited to what he heard around the watercooler and to specific assignments Fluck asked him to undertake. To put it bluntly, he had no control over the direction of the investigation in the beginning. Even though he was involved in the interview process, he was still a bit player. He ached to get off the bench and into the game.

To keep his growing curiosity at bay, Morgan sought information from people in the know, the people closest to the case. He hung out in the break room, near the coffeemaker, in the hallway, anywhere he could catch a detective who was working more directly on the case. He picked their brains, asked for their hypotheses, and drew conclusions of his own that he kept to himself.

He started to see a pattern of growing frustration among the investigators who were working diligently on the case. They shared with him their concerns that Ann Miller seemed untouchable despite their best efforts to see her. She seemed to create nothing but obstacles for detectives at every turn.

Morgan wanted to be involved in the case so badly he could taste it. It was all he thought about day and night. But police protocol dictated that he stay out of it. Luckily, Morgan was never a person who cared much for protocol.

The more he learned from his own interviews and from his coworkers, the more he was convinced that he knew what had happened; maybe not all of the details, but that would come later. He knew enough to know that a killer was roaming the streets, free and clear. A killer who might just get away with murder if something wasn't done to turn up the heat on the investigation.

•

The biggest problem was the Raleigh Police Department's lack of access to Ann Miller. Her high-powered attorney, Wade Smith, kept promising she would come down to the station for an interview, but Morgan knew it wouldn't happen. Wade Smith was an unfailingly polite and gracious man. In jest, he often called himself a country lawyer, but had an uptown practice with a price tag to match. He spoke with an educated lilt that made him sound more like an Ivy League college professor than an attorney. It was Morgan's understanding that Smith was going to try to get Ann Miller to come down to the station for another interview, but it never happened.

"I don't really know what Ann told him," Morgan says, always willing to give a star attorney like Smith the benefit of the doubt, "but I think she told him enough, even if she didn't tell him the whole truth, so that he realized it would certainly not be in her best interest to actually cooperate with the police."

THE E-MAIL TRAIL

People are often still naively unaware, even with today's advanced technology, that almost anything you delete from a computer can be retrieved. But this lack of clarity about what is accessible and what is not serves investigators well. It allows them to gather information they would never have had access to before.

The e-mail trail that Ann Miller recklessly left in her wake was the first solid lead in the case. When her computer records started coming in, investigators got a better picture of what had *really* been going on in Ann Miller's life. According to Morgan, a cop who was just learning how to maneuver around a computer himself, this information was probably the most damning circumstantial evidence he had ever come across in all of his gritty years in investigations.

Like most cops, Morgan worked off-duty security to make a few extra bucks. It was a practice the department not only allowed, but endorsed. After all, who could support a family on a cop's salary? One night while on one of his off-duty jobs, Morgan grabbed a stack of the e-mails investigators had collected in the Miller case and started reading.

"What we found on Eric Miller's computer was about as pure as the driven snow," says Morgan, who'd expected as much. Eric's e-mail communications were "vanilla" in nature, either work-related, or if they were personal, mainly focused on his baby daughter, Clare. There was nothing in Eric's e-mail to suggest that he had problems in his marriage, nothing to suggest that he suspected his wife of infidelity. In fact there was nothing to suggest a conflict with anyone at all.

For Morgan this was a key element because it showed that Eric Miller never saw anything coming. He had no idea that someone had put a target on his forehead. That's why, even when he lay dying in a hospital bed, he would never have suspected that someone had poisoned him.

In addition to searching Eric Miller's computer, investigators searched his lab. There was no arsenic anywhere to be found. Clearly, this meant that the arsenic poisoning had not been the result of an accidental exposure. Something Morgan had always thought unlikely, but now the theory was finally disqualified.

As soon as Morgan began reading the records from Ann's computers, however, he got a very different picture of the allegedly loving spouse and now grieving widow. He discovered that Ann had a fantasy life so rich, so well crafted, that it had almost replaced her real life. The more he read, the more the inner workings of this woman's mind amazed him.

Ann had a flirtatious online correspondence with a coworker at Glaxo Wellcome named Derril Willard. There was nothing in the e-mails that jumped out and stated in black and white that Ann Miller and Derril Willard were involved in a romantic relationship, but according to Morgan, it was pretty clear from the tenor of the messages that one existed. He also knew that Ann was too smart to make her e-mails *too* obvious. Morgan said reading the exchanges was like hearing half of a conversation. The e-mails were filled with innuendo and private jokes that only the two of them could understand and clearly had to be based on earlier conversations the couple had had in person or over the phone.

It just so happened that Willard was also one of the three men who had accompanied Eric Miller to the bowling alley on November 15, 2000. That was the night Eric got violently ill and had to be rushed to Rex Hospital the first time after vomiting and complaining of severe stomach pains.

Morgan said investigators were hoping to find a "magic bullet" in these e-mail communications. They didn't find it, but what they did find confirmed their suspicions that Ann Miller wasn't the demure, conservative, religious woman she appeared to be. It wasn't *magic,* but it was enough to begin to build a homicide case against her. Or so Morgan thought at the time. Little did he know just how rocky the road to justice would prove to be.

DIAMONDS ARE A GIRL'S BEST FRIEND

On November 15 at 10:15 a.m., just hours before the bowling outing that Eric would attend with Derril Willard, Ann Miller sent Willard an e-mail full of flowery prose worthy of a greeting-card writer. As she talked about feelings, it was almost like Ann was manipulating him with her sappy language—telling him that his "beautiful blue eyes" stirred her soul, urging him not to fear crying, that his tears were like a diamond necklace around her neck, and insisting that while occasionally confusing, "emotions are awesome." *"I want to touch you in places that you knew not existed. Take you to places you've never been before. One thing I'll never do is make you feel not wanted,"* she wrote.

Morgan strongly believed that Eric Miller got sick for the first time that fateful night at the bowling alley because someone gave him arsenic, probably in his beer. Given the apparent connection between Ann Miller and Derril Willard, it seemed likely that Ann had coerced Willard into participating in her evil scheme. In Morgan's mind it was clear that in the e-mail Ann was greasing the wheel, buttering up Willard for what he was about to do, what she had asked and prodded him to do. Morgan believed even then, in the early stages of the investigation, that Ann used her power over Willard to rope him into a plot to kill her husband.

And yet despite a lot of innuendo in the e-mails between Ann and Willard, the so-called magic bullet was still elusive. There was nothing concrete in the electronic transmissions linking the two directly, or even indirectly, to Eric's death.

"There was nothing talking about how Eric is a bad person, there was nothing talking about 'let's get rid of Eric and be together forever,'" says Morgan.

CALIFORNIA DREAMING

Derril Willard was not Ann Miller's only e-mail pal. Police also found e-mails between Ann and a man named Carl Mackewicz, a scientist she had worked with from San Francisco. He later became known as "Carl M." to detectives who did not want to go to the trouble of correctly pronouncing his last name. From what investigators uncovered, Ann had a long-standing, long-distance relationship with Mackewicz dating back to 1997. It was a relationship that apparently continued throughout her marriage, a relationship that Eric Miller may or may not have known about. Morgan suspected that even if Eric had had an inkling, his concerns were quickly allayed by excuses and lies from Ann. Morgan was beginning to realize that Ann was cavalier, a risk taker to whom men were a sport, and it was a game she excelled at playing.

"They [the e-mails] talked about really what I think you can describe as Ann's fantasy world. The woman, for all of her faults, does have a vivid imagination," Morgan says, paying Ann Miller a very rare compliment.

In the early days of the investigation, Morgan says that Mackewicz repeatedly denied the affair with Ann Miller, a denial that would later come back to haunt him. Raleigh police detective Doug Brugger made an unannounced visit to San Francisco, where he confronted Mackewicz face-to-face. But Mackewicz wouldn't budge. He refused to admit that there was anything more than a friendship between himself and Ann.

But e-mails don't lie, and there's nothing truly private in cyberspace. Later, after many conversations with detectives on the phone, it would be these e-mails that would push Mackewicz to admit his real relationship with Ann Miller.

On November 22, 2000, at 1:24 in the afternoon, while Eric Miller was seriously ill and lying in a bed at UNC Hospital, Mackewicz wrote to Ann. It was clear in the e-mail that Mackewicz knew nothing about Eric Miller's illness. The tone was lighthearted as he asked about getting an invitation to Ann's Christmas party and cashing in on an earlier promise for a glass of wine shared at a beach house in front of a warm fire.

On November 23, 2000, at 8:55 in the morning, Ann responded that she had stopped off at the office for a moment.

She described her husband's illness as "deathly" and explained what a burden it was taking care of him, her daughter, and dealing with her in-laws at the same time. "I'd throw my own Christmas party if I thought you would come. I'd buy a house at the beach too. I could so use a friend," she wrote. She urged him to call her at the house and said it was safe because her in-laws were "oblivious" to who was calling her.

This particular e-mail stuck in Morgan's head and would later haunt him when hearing about the antics of Scott Peterson as his wife lay dead beneath the murky, cold waters of San Francisco Bay. Morgan couldn't shake the fact that while Eric lay dying, Ann was flirting online with another man in such a casual manner. It didn't prove that she killed him, but it sure didn't point to her innocence either. Quite the contrary. It wasn't normal behavior for a woman who was supposed to be keeping a vigil by her sick husband's bedside, but by this time Morgan had started to realize that very little about Ann Miller was normal.

Investigators also found another interesting document on Ann's computer. She had written a short story called "96 Hours—the West Edge." Morgan would later discover that the story was a fictionalized version of a romantic weekend Ann Miller had shared with Carl Mackewicz.

The passage was dated July 30, 1998, and was written in the first person. "I had an uneasy feeling about being there— but at the same time excited," Ann wrote. She described the man in the story as sporting a few days of stubble, something that made him look rumpled and attractive, and the woman in the story wondered whether she and the man had similar thoughts about what the weekend would bring. They packed for a camping trip to the Redwoods, a place called Camp Meeker, and when they arrived they set up camp in front of the heater on the floor of the cabin. Then, "He told me where he hoped things would go—a bold gesture on my behalf but admirable he said. I wanted the same . . ." she wrote.

The e-mail trail revealed that Ann and Mackewicz had met in San Francisco, Lake Tahoe, New York, and the Outer Banks—all without Eric's knowledge. At this point Morgan knew they were not dealing with an ordinary woman, but with someone who had a powerful ability to manipulate the people around her, maybe even the police. In all of his years as an investigator, Morgan had never encountered someone quite like Ann Miller, someone with the power and grace to manipulate almost any situation, any person. He vowed right then and there that *he* would not be manipulated by her.

Eric Miller's life insurance policy would pay a mere $100,000. Even a person of little means would know this kind of money didn't go very far. So if Ann Miller did kill her husband, it was certainly not for money. The policy wouldn't pay for her fantasy life, that's for sure. Morgan kept rolling the motive around his mind like a numbered Ping-Pong ball in a lottery cage. As he read and reread the e-mails, it would have been easy to think Ann had killed her husband for another man, or even other *men*. But Morgan was convinced this was not the case. In his opinion Ann Miller wasn't that simple. Her motive was not one that could easily be discerned using the logic of a normal person because she *wasn't* a normal person.

"I think she killed Eric so that she could fully explore and experience the kind of life that she fantasized and imagined," says Morgan as he looks wistfully out the window in his study, ignoring the barking dog in the distance.

It was a life Morgan was determined to make sure that Ann Miller never got a chance to enjoy.

"ANN TIME"

In black Magic Marker on the dry-erase board where investigators listed facts about the case, Morgan clearly remembers one phrase jumping out at him: ANN TIME. It came from an interview that Detective Debbie Regentin had conducted with a woman who'd attended a marriage preparation course Ann and Eric had taught at St. Francis of Assisi, the Catholic church they belonged to in Raleigh.

The very fact that a woman whose marriage was such a sham was teaching this course in the first place struck Morgan as yet further confirmation that Ann was a master of deception. But at the same time it made sense because it helped complete the image that the Millers were so happy and in sync with each other that they wanted to share their joy with others about to enter into holy matrimony.

Apparently, Ann told the woman that one of the major things she missed and had sacrificed in order to be a wife and a mother was having time to herself. According to Morgan,

Ann admitted to the woman that she was remorseful about letting go of her personal time in order to fulfill her responsibilities at home. She even complained that Eric was not a full partner in child-rearing or housekeeping duties.

"Apparently this lack of 'Ann Time' had had a profound effect on Ann," says Morgan with more than a hint of disgust in his voice.

None of this information jibed with what other people had told detectives. Family, friends, and neighbors all said that the Millers were a happy couple with normal marital issues, but nothing that would raise red flags. In fact Morgan was told by numerous people that Eric was more than a part-time contributor when it came to household chores and taking care of baby Clare, that he often pitched in to do more than his share and in the process lightened Ann's load significantly.

Morgan said Eric would always drop off Clare at Bright Horizons day care in the morning and that Ann would pick her up in the afternoons. Day-care employees told investigators that because of the flexible schedule he had as a researcher, Eric would drop off Clare late in the mornings so that he could spend a couple of hours with her first. To Morgan, Eric sounded like a doting father and husband.

While it may not have been clear to everyone at this point, a motive was starting to form in Morgan's mind. Two simple words—"Ann Time."

TWO

*Facts do not cease to exist
because they are ignored.*
—ALDOUS HUXLEY

"I liked the doctor at first, but later I didn't like her any-more," Ann Miller told Detectives Debbie Regentin and Randy Miller that first night in the interview room as she cried in between her words. She was describing Eric's experience at Rex Hospital just before he was moved to UNC Hospital.

"Doctor?" the detective asked.

"Mohan. She said he's going to die, he'll be dead," Ann said.

"Who did she tell that? The day that he left Rex?" the detective followed up.

"Yes. I didn't know if I should move him or not and I didn't want him to have to go through all that. Again he [Eric] told me he can't do that anymore, he said, 'I don't want to get up and go through all of that again, because I can't go through all the doctors,' and he said 'Ann, I want

33

to be here,' the doctor really recommended it and said what we should do is move him," Ann said.

"Why did she say he was going to die?" the detective asked.

"I don't know," Ann said.

"Did she tell you why she thought that?" he said.

"Because his heart function was low, and if he was going to need a transplant," Ann uttered once again sobbing, "that they wanted [him] to go over there and they wanted to move him before he was too weak. They didn't wait. They had done a bone marrow and they did a CAT scan and a sigmoidoscope and they put him on drugs that I told them not to. They wouldn't, they weren't listening to me. He went crazy one night and they had to tie him down."

Snippets from Ann's police interview that first night continued to permeate Morgan's brain. What she said, how she said it, what she didn't say. He couldn't shake the feeling that the clues were all there; he just had to put them in some kind of order.

For example, UNC Hospitals in Chapel Hill did a second set of heavy-metals testing on Eric Miller when he was moved there from Rex Hospital on November 21, though the results weren't returned immediately. Eric was discharged from UNC on November 24 and appeared to be getting better. But when Eric became violently ill with the same symptoms and was readmitted to Rex on December 1, a doctor from UNC called the Miller house to tell Ann that the test results were finally back from Eric's previous stay at UNC and that they were *positive* for arsenic. Ann gave the UNC doctor Dr. Mehna Mohan's pager number at Rex.

"Yes, when he called I told him to call Dr. Mohan. I went back to the hospital. Eric was real white. He said, 'Dr. Mohan,' she went running to him," Ann said, weeping in the interview room, "She said: 'Eric, somebody's trying to kill you.' And she told him . . . she terrified him; I can't believe she told him. How could she have done that?" Ann said, barely above a whisper.

DO YOU HEAR WHAT I HEAR?

Morgan listened to every word Ann Miller said that night, over and over, the night of her first and only interview with police. Ann's voice was so low on the tape, barely audible in fact, that it had to be sent to the State Bureau of Investigation to be enhanced. From that enhancement a transcript was made. Morgan must have read that transcript a hundred times until it was dog-eared, coffee-stained, and faded. He dissected Ann's words over and over, picking apart her story piece by piece.

When someone dies, life goes on. Morgan was acutely aware of this fact. It goes on just as furiously and frenetically as it did prior to the person's death. We would all like to believe that subtracting ourselves from the universe would topple the earth from its axis, but in reality, the world keeps spinning and so does everything else.

Within a week of Eric Miller's murder, Chris Morgan's squad had another death to investigate. Cedric Brame could not have been more different from Dr. Eric Miller. Morgan said Brame was a drug dealer, and a not a very good one at that. Brame had been given a second chance *twice* before the shooting that ended his life. Prior to this, Morgan said Brame had been shot on two other occasions and somehow miraculously lived to tell the stories. This time he was not so lucky.

"It's not a mystery that Cedric's dead," Morgan says, shaking his head. "The mystery is that he lived as long as he did."

Morgan said Cedric died the way he lived. But Eric Miller, on the other hand, lived an exemplary life by all accounts. He was a model employee, good father, son, sibling, friend, and husband. There was nothing in Eric's background to suggest that anyone would dislike him, let alone hate him enough to *kill* him.

This struck Morgan as unusual. Most victims have something in their past or present that might trigger negative reactions from others. Not Eric Miller. In Morgan's mind Eric was probably the purest example of an innocent victim he had ever encountered.

THE FAMILY TREE

Chris Morgan realized that in order to solve this murder, detectives needed to know Eric Miller *personally*. At this point Morgan was still on the outside edges of the investigation, but he eventually got to know Eric through his family, by talking to his friends and colleagues. Morgan had gotten to know many victims this way. He inhaled the small details of their lives that made them into the people they were before they were killed.

Did they wash their own cars, or go to the car wash? Did they drink diet soda or regular? Did they listen to country music or soft rock? For some people this may sound tedious; for Morgan it was his job. He may have never actually met them in life, but in some ways he knew the victims better than the people who spent their entire lives with them.

Morgan had a picture in his head of a boy growing up in Indiana in a family reminiscent of the 1950s classic *Ozzie & Harriet*. Eric Miller was from a good, sturdy Midwestern family for whom a love of God, family, and country made up the bedrock of his upbringing. Morgan had never been to Indiana, and really knew very little about the Midwest, but it's a picture that he continued to embellish upon the more he learned about Eric. Years later Morgan would look back with almost eerie clarity and realize in the end just how right he had been about Eric Miller's background.

Eric Miller was born in 1970, in Cambridge City, Indiana, to Doris and Verus Miller. It was a small town where everyone knew one other. He had two older sisters whom he equally adored, and who adored him—Pam and Leeann. Eric had attended Lincoln High School, where he was the class vice president, a standout on the tennis team, and a member of the National Honor Society. It was these snippets of information, Eric's life résumé if you will, that gave Morgan a preliminary outline of the man he would soon come to know intimately.

Miller had grown up an active member of St. Elizabeth

Catholic Church. He was an altar boy. Friends said he was popular with the girls, but he made it clear he was saving his virginity for marriage.

Eric's future wife, Ann Rene Brier, the oldest of three girls, was born on March 27, 1970, to Dan and Nancy Brier. Her sister Danielle came along in March of 1972, and Sara was born in October of 1980. Like her future husband, Ann also grew up in an all-American small town. Spring Grove, Pennsylvania, was not much different from Cambridge City, Indiana. Also like Eric, Ann was popular and athletic. She played field hockey and ran on the track team. She was even pretty enough to be a runner-up prom queen and cheerleader. Like Eric, Ann *appeared* to come from a salt-of-the-earth family.

Chris Morgan believed the end of Eric Miller's life was foreshadowed the day he met his future wife in biology class at Purdue University in West Lafayette, Indiana. They were both ambitious scientists with a desire to further their careers. Ann Brier also found another link with her future spouse—they shared a rare blood type, Rh negative. Medical experts say unless both parents have this same, uncommon blood type, there can be complications during pregnancy.

"I still marvel sometimes at the ability and guts Ann had to try and pull off some of the things she did," says Morgan. To this day he still doesn't know how or if this "compatibility factor" motivated Ann Miller, but he knew enough about her to realize that Ann rarely did anything without a clear and direct goal in mind.

Morgan says that soon after meeting, the pair became a couple. Eric proposed to Ann on Valentine's Day in 1992, and as planned, she accepted. That same year they both graduated from Purdue with honors and degrees in biology. Father John Luerman married Ann and Eric on February 27, 1993, in the Catholic church Eric had attended as a child. They then migrated to the Raleigh area to pursue doctoral degrees at North Carolina State University. Another lure—Ann's parents were living in Raleigh, where her mother was a teacher's assistant and her father worked for the John Deere Company.

The couple bought their first house in the suburbs in a quaint bedroom community of Raleigh called Holly Springs, a town that was not unlike the modest, wholesome tree-lined communities where they had both grown up. They were living the American dream; at least that's what it looked like to the outside world.

Eric was described to Morgan by fellow students and teachers as a bright self-starter, devoted to his work, his wife, and his church. Ann, on the other hand, did not do as well in her doctoral program as Eric, and ultimately dropped out to take a job with Glaxo Wellcome (now GlaxoSmithKline), a large pharmaceutical company in the business sector of Raleigh called Research Triangle Park.

The couple bought a new home in West Raleigh in September of 1997. Eric graduated with a doctorate in 1999 and started work as an AIDS researcher at UNC–Chapel Hill's Lineberger Comprehensive Cancer Center. With his new job, the pair was ready to start a family, but despite their compatible blood types, their road to fertility was not smooth. After months of trying unsuccessfully to conceive a child, they eventually attempted in vitro fertilization.

In an e-mail to Carl Mackewicz on January 21, 1999, Ann Miller shared her fertility struggles with him. "I have been through so many Dr.'s and nurses you couldn't begin to imagine . . . I decided by giving up hope—I'd be taking the middle road—I wouldn't be setting myself and my family up for disappointment constantly," said Ann.

She went on to describe how her feelings about her fertility struggles had caused her to be resentful of her family. Although she says she felt guilty about having these thoughts, "It's difficult to even see my sister there holding her child—I feel envy, hurt and could even go as far to say disgust," she wrote.

Finally, the fertility treatments took. On January 17, 2000, Clare Elise Miller came into the world at Rex Hospital. Morgan cannot talk about this event in the Miller time line without reminding anyone who is listening that this is the same hospital where Clare's father would die less than a year after his daughter's birth. Clare's well-being became a driving force for Morgan and the entire Miller family early on in the investigation into Eric's murder. In fact, she was such a driving force, that Morgan's desire to tell this story comes largely from his desire for Clare to know the truth.

Morgan and many other investigators talked to Eric's neighbors, coworkers, and friends. Everyone described Eric Miller as funny, full of life, a wonderful father. He loved children so much he even made special bags for the neighborhood kids on Halloween. He loved the outdoors and was especially at home in the garden. He was what Morgan referred to as a "meat-and-potatoes guy." In the hundreds of interviews that were done, Morgan insists that not one person had a negative thing to say about Eric Miller. This simply doesn't happen in murder investigations. Not one negative comment, snide remark, or qualified statement? If Eric had any skeletons in his closet, Morgan never found them; and Morgan was good at finding skeletons.

The more Morgan learned, the more he was convinced that Ann Miller was putting on an act. She pretended to be the devoted wife and loving mother, but she was something else altogether. She was a woman he felt sure was capable of killing her husband even if he didn't have the proof yet.

SILVER BELLS

Over the Christmas holidays that first year, less than a month after Eric's death, Ann packed up nearly one-year-old baby Clare and headed to Indiana to spend time with Eric's family. When Morgan heard about this he could not believe the gall of the woman. He was frightened by her amazing ability to appear so convincingly innocent to everyone around her. If she was truly responsible for her husband's murder, this was a dangerous game of manipulation. By allowing herself to be cocooned in the center of the family that was so desperately grieving Eric's loss, she was risking being found out. But Morgan would soon come to understand that risk taking was a large part of Ann Miller's personality.

In Morgan's mind the holiday visit made it even less likely that the police would consider Ann a suspect in her husband's death. It was part of a very simple and seemingly perfect plan. Clearly, one would imagine that a murderer wouldn't dare spend time with the family of the man whom she had killed. It didn't make sense. And because it didn't make sense, this simple act helped cast her as the grieving widow in the eyes of the world instead of as a cold-blooded killer.

FOR THE LOVE OF ERIC

When Doris and Verus Miller came to Raleigh for their son's funeral, they had no inkling that their daughter-in-law might be a suspect. They were operating under a cloud of grief and shock so thick that they could hardly see in front of them. In most murder cases Morgan noticed that grief had a way of sucking people into a dark place that they must claw their way out of. Sometimes this took years. Because of their all-consuming grief, it was impossible for them to see a potential killer in their inner circle, the mother of their grandchild, the woman who had promised to love and cherish their son.

Morgan recalls first meeting the Millers in passing when they came to the police station in January of 2001. They were in town along with their daughters, Eric's sisters, Pam and Leeann, to help celebrate baby Clare's first birthday. It was clear to Morgan that maintaining a relationship with their granddaughter was akin to staying connected to their dead son. Captain Donald Overman was the officer tasked with speaking to the Millers during their brief visit. After the meeting he voiced his concerns to Morgan.

"Overman came out of the meeting and said, 'We've got to do something for these people. They don't have a clue. They don't have any idea what's going on here,' " Morgan says.

It was then that Morgan vowed that he would not let the Millers be manipulated by a woman who he believed with all his heart had something to do with their son's death. But the timing had to be right; Morgan didn't want to spook Ann too early by letting it slip that the police were onto her already. He knew that the Millers' close relationship with Ann might benefit the investigation down the road. Years later he would revisit this notion and realize just how important this seemingly small detail had become to the big picture.

MAGICAL THINKING

Dr. Michael Teague, the forensic psychologist for the Raleigh Police Department, was often Morgan's "partner in crime." They batted about theories like friendly rivals on a tennis court firing balls at each other, though it was clear neither of them had been on an actual tennis court for a very long time, if ever. They didn't always agree, but Morgan consistently sought Teague's input, if for no other reason than to give him another angle to consider.

Teague was convinced that Ann Miller was living in a delusional state of mind he labeled "magical thinking." Basically Teague thought Ann felt herself to be so superior to everyone around her, especially police officers, that she completely denied any possibility that she risked being found out. The image that she had fashioned for the world—of a loving wife, doting mother, and esteemed scientist—was what she saw when she looked in the mirror, and she magically assumed that everyone else saw the same thing.

By this time investigators had enough evidence to safely conclude that Ann Miller had had affairs with Carl Mackewicz and Derril Willard. Morgan thought for sure that when Ann suspected that the heat was on her, she would turn on one or both of these men and possibly blame them for Eric's murder. At the very least, Morgan assumed Ann would come clean early on in the investigation in order to try to spin the affairs to her advantage in some way, to couch herself in the guise of a naive woman who'd been led astray. But she said nothing, and her lawyers said nothing.

In January of 2001, Ann Miller retained a second high-powered attorney, Joseph Cheshire, who, like Ann's other attorney, Wade Smith, later became well known for defending one of the Duke lacrosse players against allegations of rape. Again, like Smith, Cheshire was a formidable force in the world of defense attorneys. The fact that Ann had hired not one, but two heavy hitters was another huge red flag for Morgan. In North Carolina people who faced the death penalty were always given two court-appointed attorneys if they could not afford to pay for their own. Morgan wondered if Ann was planning ahead.

Morgan kept going back to the transcript from the single time Ann had been interviewed by police. That night offered the only peek directly into Ann's state of mind. At this point in the game it was all Morgan had to hang his big white fedora on.

"While the detectives that interviewed her that night never did ask her point-blank, 'Did you kill your husband?' one thing they did ask her, and that was a good question, was, 'Do you know of anybody who had anything against Eric?' " Morgan recalled from the transcript. Ann had answered in a roundabout way, saying that Eric had had a minor dispute with a neighbor over a privacy fence, but it was clear that this altercation wouldn't have risen to the level of murder.

Morgan always thought Ann had missed a perfect opportunity that night to point the finger at Willard and set the stage early on for him to take the fall. But she didn't. To Morgan, Ann Miller was not nearly as smart as the woman she saw looking back at her in the mirror.

MEDICAL MYSTERY

Morgan recalls that about this time medical records were starting to pour in. What they showed was that Eric Miller had made a remarkable recovery after being released from UNC Hospitals on November 24, before he was readmitted to Rex Hospital on December 1, where he ultimately died. All of the reports showed that during this period of time Eric Miller's health was on the upswing. Doctors told investigators that most people exposed to high doses of arsenic either die immediately or recover fully.

"Eric's case didn't fit the pattern. He got exposed to arsenic, he improved, and then all of a sudden he became terribly, terribly ill again at a time that coincided with him essentially being alone with Ann," Morgan said.

Investigators learned that on November 30, the night before his final hospitalization at Rex, Eric was alone with Ann at their home. Verus and Doris, who had been in town since Eric's first hospitalization, had gone out to dinner alone for the first time in a week. Ann had warmed up a chicken-and-rice dish that someone from their church had bought over for her and Eric. A little more than twenty-four hours after his last meal with Ann, Eric Miller was dead.

By this time investigators had also noted that Derril Willard was very much out of the running as someone who could have administered the last, deadly dose of arsenic to Eric. He had had no contact with Eric Miller since that night at the bowling alley some two weeks prior. The *only* person who had close contact with Eric Miller the night before his downward spiral into eventual death was his wife.

"The whole situation started to very much fall under 'the truth makes sense,'" says Morgan. "If it doesn't make sense, it's probably not true. It had a smell about it. It had a slight smell that first night. As time went on, the smell got even more and more pronounced."

THREE

He who truly knows has no need to shout.
—LEONARDO DA VINCI

"I searched your house and in the trash can I found a note that you wrote," Detective Debbie Regentin stated to Ann in that first and only interview with her. "Do you know when it was written?"

"No, I don't remember. Eric always kept them. I would tear them up," Ann said matter-of-factly.

"In another note I found you had written that Eric was wanting you to give up a friend. I know you guys are professional people. Do you remember the note?" the detective countered Ann's dismissal of the issue.

"Eric was overly jealous," Ann said of her dead husband. "Ninety percent of the people I work with are men."

"Like my work," Detective Regentin responded without judgment.

"He has a hard time with that. I have a very good friend

at work. I have a lot of friends at work. I think the friend was a guy in California. I worked on a project with him. He showed me around while I was there. Eric asked me not to spend so much time with him," Ann said with a hint of annoyance in her voice.

"You were just friends?" the detective asked.

Ann Miller never answered the question. But investigators would soon learn the answer. The letter was about Carl Mackewicz, and based on what they learned, he was much more than just a *friend* to Ann Miller.

IT TAKES TWO

Early on in the investigation, Chris Morgan felt that detectives should focus on whether or not Ann had had help killing Eric, even if her accomplice may not have been part of the final act. Clearly, she had questionable relationships with multiple men. Carl Mackewicz or Derril Willard *might* have been in on her plan. But even if neither of them physically helped her, it's unlikely that she kept her evil deeds entirely to herself. In Morgan's experience, killers often felt the need to tell someone what they had done. The catharsis of telling even just one person was often the key to solving the case. In Morgan's mind that one person might just be Derril Willard.

As investigators looked at the events surrounding the night at the bowling alley on November 15, 2000, the night Eric became violently ill and was first hospitalized, it became clear that he must have received a dose of arsenic in his beer. Eric had told the men he was with that the beer tasted funny and almost immediately afterward started having violent stomach pains. Ann Miller, the good wife, the concerned wife, took her husband to Rex Hospital early in the morning on November 16.

"Within two hours of arriving at the bowling alley, he was throwing up in a bag, in a garbage can, while he was still trying to bowl," says Morgan. "Within two hours of drinking that beer, the symptoms of arsenic poisoning started to fully manifest themselves in Eric Miller."

THE GOOD WIFE

"He started throwing up about eleven," a tearful Ann told the detective. "And then he was throwing up until the wee hours, and he always, it makes him mad when I say this, but Eric always gets sick worse than Clare and I. He always gets it harder," Ann said, sobbing.

"He got up every hour on the hour at three like he had thought maybe he should go to the hospital but he didn't want to wake Clare, so at six he said I'm not going to be okay. I got dressed and I got Clare and we went to the emergency room that morning."

The detective went on to ask Ann Miller whether or not her husband ate or drank anything at the house before going to the hospital. She told him that she gave Eric a Coke.

"They admitted him. They said he had that stomach flu," Ann told the detective. "Two or three nurses had gone home from it. And it comes from something you eat and then he got very distended and he said help me because he wanted, he wanted to be helped. He went back in X-ray. He had fluids around his heart and then they left him in the ER. They told him he was going to get a room for his stomach flu. He was in the ER for thirty hours. I came back. I'm getting mad at the ER because he is still there. He said, 'You go home,'" Ann said, pausing for a moment. "He said, 'You go home and get some rest,' and I came back the next morning and he was still there," she said, sobbing again. "He was still looking pale in the ER and he couldn't sleep and nobody called me because he was all alone and all that noise. The doctor came in and she got really mad. She said the nurses are terrible, and the doctor got really mad he was still there."

TRUTH-SEEKING

Morgan was mad on so many levels. He was mad that Eric Miller had died. He was mad that Eric Miller might not have had the best care at the end of his life. He was mad that the woman Eric Miller trusted the most, his wife, might be responsible for his death.

Morgan wanted to know more about the group Miller went bowling with, particularly Derril Willard, in light of the romantic e-mails Willard had exchanged with Ann and Eric's sudden illness at the bowling alley. If Willard had helped Ann, even if he had had second thoughts when the notion of killing an innocent man became too much for him to bear, then he was still the investigators' best bet for getting someone to turn on Ann. If Willard knew something, if they could get him to talk, the case would be solved, over, done. But these were a whole lot of ifs.

Phone records started to dribble into the police department in mid-December after police made official requests to the wireless carriers. Like the e-mails, they showed an unmistakable pattern of communication between Ann and Willard. They revealed that Willard and Ann had called each other more than one hundred times between October 30, 2000, and December 2, 2000, the day of Eric's death. Ann called Willard seventy-nine times. He called her just thirty-eight times. They talked for a total of an astounding 576 minutes. These were all just numbers, but important numbers to Morgan, numbers that added up to two things: an ongoing romantic affair, and possibly an accomplice in Eric Miller's death.

They called each other at all hours of the day and night and talked for long periods of time. One twenty-four-minute call came just two hours before Eric Miller died. Then the calls abruptly stopped. In Morgan's mind either Willard knew Ann had killed her husband and ended the communication himself, or more likely, Ann ended it because she had no more use for him.

It didn't take a brilliant scientist to figure out this one. Morgan presumed Ann had been having an affair with Willard in order to gain his trust so that he would in turn help her kill Eric. Again, as Morgan believed that Ann never did anything without a purpose, he felt there had to be a core motivation behind the affair other than pleasure or insecurity. After all, she already had Carl Mackewicz, and who knows how many other men. Did she really need another lover?

And there was more—police found two hundred milliliters of an arsenic compound called sodium cacodylate in the lab where Ann and Willard worked at Glaxo Wellcome. They were told that this was a typical amount for the lab to stock on a daily basis. After consulting with experts, investigators learned that this amount of the compound was easily enough to kill someone. Although such evidence was all still circumstantial, proving that Ann and Willard had access to the poison that killed Eric it was *very strong* circumstantial evidence. In addition, investigators discovered that at the time Eric was killed there was no routine inventory taken, nor was there a system to monitor who was taking what from the lab.

All three of the men who attended the bowling outings were colleagues of Ann's from Glaxo Wellcome. Very quickly investigators were able to catch up with two of them and interview them. Randy Bledsoe and Tom Councilor talked to the police; only Derril Willard proved elusive. To be honest, though, police were not exactly chasing Willard down. A month after Eric's death, Sergeant Fluck told Morgan they were still trying to set up an interview with Willard and had left messages at his office, but hadn't done anything else to pursue a face-to-face meeting. Morgan was astounded that they had not tried harder to pin Willard down.

"In my way of thinking, it was a mistake," Morgan says. "I would have been sitting with my fat butt on Willard's car every day." And he means it.

Not unlike the way he got to know his victims, Morgan wanted to learn everything he could about Derril Willard so that he might understand how the man was caught up in Ann Miller's complicated web of deceit. In his gut he suspected that Willard might be a victim as well, a victim of Ann Miller's charm and powers of seduction, an unwitting partner in a plot to kill a good man. Morgan needed Willard's help to unravel the web.

THE TURNING POINT

In late January, the men in charge of the investigation, Sergeant Jeff Fluck and Lieutenant Gerald Britt, were out of town. Captain Donald Overman was left to tend to the case in their absence. After meeting with Eric Miller's family on January 19, 2001, Morgan said Overman became concerned that the investigation was lagging— that Derril Willard could be holding the key to the entire case, yet no one had made any real effort to get him to talk.

Morgan reasons that Fluck probably didn't want to push Willard because he might have gotten scared and "lawyered up," an expression for hiring a lawyer and shutting out the police. But still, it was clear to Morgan that without Willard the case could not move forward. Yet he knew that Fluck was right; Willard was a bright scientist, and chances were he was smart enough to know that his relationship with Ann had gotten him into real trouble.

"We got to get a statement from this guy, even if he

lies," Morgan said. "You have to expect that he's going to lie, but you have to nail him down and stake him out."

Again, it still wasn't officially Morgan's case. But as luck would have it, he was on duty that week, and Captain Overman needed a supervisor to oversee a search of Willard's home. This is how Morgan says he got "pulled into the investigation through no fault of his own." But it wasn't like he put up a fight.

Detective Randy Miller drew up a search warrant in order to obtain legal probable cause from a judge to enter Willard's home. At the same time, Morgan was strategizing about how to approach Willard. Even more of a concern was knowing that as soon as the search warrant was returned to the Wake County Magistrate's Office, the media would get a hold of it. Key details of the case that investigators had been keeping under wraps for several weeks would suddenly become part of the public record.

This thought would stick with Morgan for years like gum that he couldn't scrape off the bottom of his shoe. He knew that a talented local newspaper reporter for the *News and Observer*, Oren Dorell, was a well-known "search-warrant grazer," who would find the information and put it on the front page of the newspaper above the fold for everyone to see.

The search warrant contained information about the bowling outing, what was thought to be arsenic in the beer, and the romantic relationship between Ann and Willard. Specifically, it stated that the two other men at the bowling alley that night saw Willard purchase the beer and pour cups for everyone with the exception of one man who did not drink. This meant that the cup of beer that Eric drank from went directly from Willard's hands to Eric's lips. While the warrant didn't spell it out, the obvious conclusion that anyone reading the warrant would draw was that Willard must have put the arsenic in Eric's beer.

Based on this information, Morgan wanted to arrest Willard for attempted murder. It occurred to Morgan that if the police had enough probable cause to search Willard's home, they had enough probable cause to arrest him. In fact, Morgan considered this the right thing to do. It would put Willard where they wanted and needed him—behind bars, in their custody, and hopefully willing to bargain for his freedom with the truth. But again, his wishes fell on deaf ears. Morgan says the assistant Wake County district attorney handling the case, Tom Ford, did not believe there was enough evidence to charge Willard and that a premature arrest could irrevocably damage the case.

"To say that I perceived Tom Ford as a developing problem in this case is a huge understatement. I mean Tom Ford *was* the problem in this case initially," states Morgan.

Investigators in Wake County were used to working closely with prosecutors. With few exceptions, cops didn't make arrests in serious cases without the approval of the district attorney. Prosecutors also had a different standard; probable cause wasn't enough. Before an arrest in a high-profile case, they wanted to make sure there was enough to convict someone beyond a reasonable doubt in front of a jury. Morgan didn't always like the process, but he understood how it worked and had come to accept it. Morgan was beginning to worry that a case might never be made against anyone in Eric Miller's death.

Morgan believes that part of Ford's reluctance stemmed from having difficulty dealing with the medical examiner, Dr. Thomas Clark, who seemed to be perpetually putting Ford off. Clark was in charge of Eric's autopsy, and would be the key witness if the case ever went to trial. Dr. Clark would be the one to testify as to Eric's cause of death. But at this point, Morgan says, neither investigators, nor Ford and his colleagues at the D.A.'s office, had been able to get straight answers from the medical examiner.

"He [Clark] played with them, he put them off. And Jeff [Fluck] and even more so Tom Ford could not believe he was actually treating them this way," Morgan said. "I've dealt with Clark before and I knew how he was. The thing is he likes to play that game. He likes to make sure that you know he's smarter than you are, which you know in my case, I was perfectly willing to admit."

Morgan says Ford was not as willing to play Clark's game, and as a result, a standoff that almost derailed the investigation occurred early on.

In Morgan's mind everyone, but especially Tom Ford, was approaching the case from the perspective of the legal hurdles it would pose down the road.

"You can't investigate homicides on that basis," Morgan says indignantly. "The investigation of killing another human being has a rhythm of its own and . . . it can't be neatly categorized."

Morgan says that's why veteran investigators are needed to peel through the layers of a homicide case as opposed to "slick-sleeved rookies" who don't have the blood on their hands that comes from years of turning over dead bodies.

Morgan asked the question even though he knew what the answer would be. "Can't we go ahead and lock this guy up, let the chips fall?"

Under North Carolina law, officers have the right to arrest anyone if they believe there is probable cause to do so, but this doesn't mean they do it without the prosecutor's permission. Morgan has looked back on this decision countless times and wondered *what if?* What if they had arrested Willard? Would things have turned out differently?

It's a question that's haunted Morgan probably more than any other he asked himself during the entire course of the investigation. It's a question he still asks himself on a regular basis years later. But like a good soldier he followed orders and went to Willard's house with only a search warrant, *without* an arrest warrant in hand.

"I better go with the flow and do things as I've been instructed to do," says Morgan of his thought process at the time. A thought process that he later deduced was fatally flawed.

THE APPROACH

On Sunday morning January 21, 2001, all the investigators involved in the operation to confront Derril Willard met at the police station. Sergeant Fluck and Lieutenant Britt had returned to town and were told by Captain Overman that the search would take place regardless of whether or not everyone agreed it was the right course of action at this point. As a result of this perceived usurping of their power, there was a palpable feeling of tension in the air, recalls Morgan.

The plan was for Morgan and Detective Brad Kennon to head to Willard's house in North Raleigh with a team of investigators to execute the search warrant. Morgan had handpicked Kennon, one of his best detectives, to help him on this mission. Two other investigators would head to the Miller house and speak to Eric's family about what was going to happen. This move was in preparation for the fact that much of the information in the case was about to become public record as soon as the search warrant was filed, and the police did not want the Millers to be blindsided by headlines the next day.

Although it had a Raleigh mailing address, Willard's house was in the county, not in the city limits. This meant that the Wake County Sheriff's Office had jurisdiction and that a deputy would have to assist in the execution of the warrant. The latter official stationed himself down the street from the house while Morgan and Kennon pulled up in their car. It was an unmarked Crown Victoria, but they were unmistakably cops coming to call on Derril Willard.

Willard answered the door with his two-and-a-half-year-old daughter, Kelcey, wrapped around his leg. Kelcey had bright blue eyes and white-blond hair, and it was easy for Morgan to see even in that brief moment as the door opened that Willard and his daughter were closely bonded.

"She was just a little angel terribly intimidated by my large rotund self standing at the door," Morgan says with a somber touch of humor.

Kelcey wasn't the only one who was intimidated. Morgan saw something in Willard's eyes, something he will never forget, and something he now wishes he had paid more attention to at the time. Not unlike the detectives who interviewed Ann Miller that one and only time, Morgan never realized he would get only this one crack at Willard.

"He had the look, very much, of a man who expected to be handcuffed and taken to jail. And I've often looked back and thought in retrospect, what would have happened in this case if I had followed my first instinct, if I had not been afraid of starting a firestorm?" Morgan says. "Because I think he was starting, for lack of a better term, [to] wake up and smell the coffee. I agree arresting Derril Willard that morning would have been pushing the envelope, but I still believe in my heart of hearts it would have gotten a positive result."

But as Morgan hadn't been given the authority to arrest him, even if Willard had offered his wrists to be handcuffed and said he was ready to go, there would have been nothing Morgan could have done.

So instead of making an arrest, Morgan explained to Willard that they needed to search the house, but first they wanted to have a word with him alone in the Crown Vic. Morgan specifically told Willard that they needed to speak with him out of the presence of his wife. Willard asked no questions about why they were there, or what they wanted to talk to him about, because surely he *knew*. He had been expecting them for some time.

Morgan pictured Willard in the days following Eric's death peeking out through his blinds to see if an unmarked police car was sitting in front of his house. He imagined Willard readjusting his rearview mirror every time he saw a blue-and-white pull in behind him on the highway, wondering if this was it. Would the cop turn on his lights and pull him over and say, "You're the guy we've been looking for. Ann Miller told us all about you"?

Another person who proabably had been expecting the police was Willard's wife, Yvette. Seconds after Morgan and Kennon arrived at the door, Yvette joined her husband in the front hallway. She stood behind him and listened as Morgan explained their intentions. Investigators would later learn that Willard had already told his wife about his relationship with Ann Miller—on December 7, 2000, just five days after Eric Miller's death. Morgan suspected that Yvette Willard also thought he might lead her husband away in handcuffs.

Willard appeared unsure whether he would be returning home. He looked anxious, pained, like a man who was carrying a very large burden on his shoulders. He asked Morgan if he would be coming back after the chat in the car. Morgan assured him that he didn't need to take his toothbrush with him, *not yet*.

Morgan claims Derril Willard was exactly what he'd pictured a midlevel researcher for a big pharmaceutical company would look like. Willard was pale, with tousled brown hair and a scraggly graying beard, an intellectual type. He wasn't the sort of guy Morgan would probably go fishing or share a beer with, but he immediately pegged Willard as a good guy who had become tangled up in something much bigger than himself, something he had no control of.

Morgan had done his research—Derril and Yvette Willard had their only child later in life than is usual, after Yvette turned forty. The stress of work combined with the energy drain of having a young child at a mature age had taken its toll on the couple. It was clear to Morgan even before it was ever confirmed that Yvette Willard already knew *something* about her husband's relationship with Ann Miller when she came to the door that day.

Willard agreed to go to the car with Morgan. He was ushered into the backseat as Morgan took his spot in the front passenger seat and then turned around to look the man in the eyes. Morgan had rehearsed this meeting many times over the previous forty-eight hours, yet what he had planned to say didn't seem right at that moment. Instead, he went off script and said the first thing that came to his mind.

"I said, 'Derril, you've been used,' " Morgan recalls. " 'I think you've been used by a woman.' Derril looked directly into my eyes and said, 'Yeah, and she's done a good job of it.' "

And then came the words every investigator dreads to hear. Derril Willard told Morgan that he could not say anything more until he talked to his attorney. Just as Sergeant Jeff Fluck had predicted, Willard had "lawyered up" and nothing else was coming out of him. As if that was not bad enough, Willard told Morgan that Rick Gammon was his attorney—another high-profile, high-priced, criminal defense attorney in Raleigh. He was a former Raleigh cop who was still admired for being able to straddle the thin blue line even as a very capable and well-respected defense attorney. Morgan and Gammon had been friends on the street when they were young beat cops on patrol. Morgan knew that Gammon wouldn't let Willard talk to them about what he had for breakfast, let alone about his love affair with Ann Miller. Gammon would protect his client at all costs.

Being the streetwise investigator that he was, Morgan just happened to have Gammon's number programmed into his cell phone, and he allowed Willard to use it to call Gammon. He was investing in the good-karma bank on the off chance that this gesture might at some point soften Willard's resolve. Morgan left Willard alone in the car so that he could have privacy. Ironically, it was this same privacy that Morgan would seek to breach years later in order to solve the case.

Morgan paced, as quickly as a large man can pace, around the perimeter of the car, ruing his misfortune and wishing he could hear what Willard was saying to Gammon behind the tinted windows of the Crown Vic. Why had all of the players in this case suddenly retained the best lawyers money could buy in Raleigh, North Carolina? He could come to only one conclusion: they had something to hide.

Morgan knew that innocent people also hired lawyers when pressured by police. But Willard had clearly hired

Gammon prior to any police pressure. Investigators would later learn that Willard had retained Gammon on December 8, 2000, just six days after Eric Miller's death. Morgan felt certain Willard had hired a lawyer because he was guilty of something; but at this point Morgan didn't know if Willard was guilty of *doing* something, or simply *knowing* something.

When Willard was done with his phone call, he told Morgan he and his family would leave the house at Gammon's advice while investigators conducted their search. Morgan was disappointed, but expected nothing less of a man represented by Rick Gammon. Gammon was a first-class attorney, someone who played by the rules, and knew how to advise his clients in tough situations. From what Morgan could tell, it didn't get any tougher than this.

COMING CLEAN

At the very same time, across town, another uncomfortable visit was taking place. Detectives had been instructed to go to the home Ann had shared with Eric in West Raleigh and speak to Verus and Doris Miller about the case. The Millers were staying with Ann as part of their January visit to celebrate Clare's first birthday.

It was decided that the time had come for the police to fill the family in on their suspicions about Ann and her possible involvement in Eric's death. Up until this time, Morgan says, the Millers had become indignant at any insinuation that Ann might be responsible for murdering their son. They defended her as strongly as they cherished Eric's memory. It was as if blaming Ann would make Eric a fool for loving her, and that was another pain the family could not bear to face.

But Captain Donald Overman decided it had to be done. He assigned detectives Debbie Regentin and Randy Miller, the same investigators who'd conducted the first interview with Ann, to go to the house and speak with Eric's parents about what police had learned so far. Regentin and Miller were the lead investigators on the case at this point, and Regentin later gave Morgan a play-by-play of what had happened at the Miller house while Morgan was on the other side of town executing the search warrant at Willard's house.

When the detectives went to the house, Doris Miller, Eric's mother, opened the door to them, but Ann, Regentin told Morgan, ran upstairs and locked herself in the bathroom with her cell phone, saying she had to call her attorney. Despite requests from Doris to come out of the bathroom, Ann vehemently refused.

Morgan was not surprised by Ann's reaction to a visit from the Raleigh police. This behavior would become a pattern with Ann when things got hard. She would go into hiding and try to wish her problems away with the "magical thinking" that allowed her to deny that she had done anything wrong. But as far as Morgan was concerned, the pressure Ann was feeling from him and the rest of the investigators would only intensify.

Investigators told Doris and Verus Miller about their suspicions—that Ann was a serial adulterer and might have had something to do with their son's death. It was an important conversation. It had to be done right. It was time to bring the Millers into the loop, to make them aware of what was going on, and at the same time solicit their help with the investigation. It was something Morgan would continue to do for years after their son's death as he forged a close bond with the family.

"I think the Millers were just aghast," Morgan said about revealing the news that Ann might be involved in Eric's death.

After several weeks of defending their daughter-in-law, it was like someone had sucked all of the oxygen out of the room and left them gasping for air. They quickly packed their belongings, left the home their dead son once shared with his now-suspect wife, and went to a hotel. Ann's parents, Dan and Nancy Brier, who lived in Raleigh, arrived to take care of Clare since Ann was still locked in the bathroom.

Ann Miller's carefully constructed fantasy world was beginning to crumble, and Morgan was smack-dab in the middle of the destruction with a pickax. But it would take years to make that one big crack that would completely open and divide that stone of fantasy.

THE BROKEN MAN

As Ann Miller's world unraveled in her bathroom, Morgan was concentrating on Derril Willard.

The thirty-seven-year-old scientist was the one person

among his immediate and extended family who had actually "made it." He was the only member of his immediate family to go to college, and certainly, the only one who became a *scientist,* of all professions.

"He was a source of great pride to his family," says Morgan.

Derril Willard was the one who escaped his small town in the foothills of the Ozarks with his sharp mind and talent, a talent that might have been buried in other people born under the same circumstances. He was the one who followed his dreams and made everyone he knew back home honored to know him.

Willard was born in 1963 in Mountain Home, Arkansas, into a strict Baptist family. He was the brightest kid anyone knew, graduating first in his class of 160 students at Batesville High School. Unlike his classmates, Willard put school, not partying or girls, first. It paid off. His good grades landed him where no one in his family had ever dared to venture before—college.

"He was the big success of his family," says Morgan.

Willard studied zoology and graduated with a master's degree from the University of Arkansas in 1988. He met his future wife, Yvette Babb, in college. They married and moved to Philadelphia, where Willard was offered a job with a pharmaceutical company. In 1990, he began working for Glaxo Wellcome in Research Triangle Park, just outside Raleigh. It was here that he met the woman who would ultimately destroy his life—Ann Miller.

THE SEARCH

In all his years of doing police work, Morgan had never gotten used to searching people's homes. Even though he believed the need to do it far outweighed the invasion of someone's personal space, it was still uncomfortable for him.

"There's just something strange about tearing through somebody else's life," Morgan admits.

They were looking for *anything* that might connect Ann and Willard to each other, or to Eric's death. Primarily, they searched Willard's home office, taking out bags of paperwork and two computers. They also searched the guest room, where it was clear that Willard had been staying. Morgan would later find out that Willard had voluntarily moved out of the master bedroom after Yvette became aware of his affair with Ann.

In addition, they searched for books or magazines that might relate to arsenic or poisoning. They found nothing, but for Morgan, the primary goal of the operation had been to meet and confront Willard face-to-face. He'd achieved that, even though there wasn't much to show for the encounter. Morgan's secondary goal was to get in and out as fast as they could without leaving the house trashed.

Investigators found three guns on a closet shelf in Willard's home. They were stored properly, out of reach of the child. At the time Morgan didn't think much about it; after all, they were looking for arsenic, not weapons. By law, if the warrant did not state that the police were looking for guns, and the guns had nothing to do with the crime, they could not be confiscated. But in hindsight, Morgan wishes he had paid more attention to this seemingly minor detail.

"The guns being there, [I] didn't really think too much about it," Morgan says. "Like I say, in retrospect I wish I had. Maybe I could have found a way—I should have just seized them."

GOOD-BYE

Derril Willard called Morgan and asked if the search was completed. Morgan told him they were almost done and he and his family could return in fifteen or twenty minutes. When Willard pulled into the garage, Morgan met him with a list of the items they had seized and explained the search in detail. Willard thanked Morgan and his officers for being so professional and not tearing the house apart.

"The pain and the angst and the fear in Derril Willard's eyes had increased," Morgan says. "He looked very much like a man on the edge to me."

For some reason Morgan could not push the memory of that meeting with Willard in the garage out of his mind. It was an unfinished garage with exposed beams in the ceiling and a small stairwell leading into the house. All Morgan could think about as he pulled away from the home that day was how easy it would be to hang yourself from a beam and jump off those steps.

"I don't know what it was, but there was something about the look in Derril Willard's eyes and something about standing there and meeting him in his garage," Morgan said with a thousand miles of unmistakable regret in his voice.

THE GOOD DOCTOR

On his way back to the police station Morgan replayed his last image of Derril Willard in his head over and over again, trying to see something that might give him more insight into Willard's subsequent behavior. He couldn't shake it. So he did what he always did in these situations. He called his colleague and good friend, police psychologist Michael Teague.

Even though Morgan refers to a lot of what Teague says as "psychobabble," he respects Teague's opinion and had sought it out frequently over the years. He especially sought it out in complicated cases like this one, where the events had taken a severe psychological and emotional toll on all of the people involved.

"I said, 'Teague, I'm not going to be a bit surprised if we find this guy dead in his garage tomorrow.'" Morgan recalls his chilling words. "Teague said, 'Why?' I said, 'He looks like he's beat, he looks like he's got no way out. He's scared and there's just nothing he can do.'"

This conversation would be one that both Morgan and Teague would remember for years to come. More than a hypothesis, it was a premonition, one that Morgan now wishes he had taken to heart.

"There's no doubt in my mind [that Willard has] been used as a pawn by this woman, Ann Miller," Morgan went on to say to Teague. "I said, 'There's really nothing we can do at this point.'"

CHANGE OF HEART

Morgan checked his voice mail on the way back to the police station. To his surprise, one of Ann Miller's colleagues, whom he had interviewed earlier in the investigation, had left him a message. It was Liping Wang. She sounded upset and told him she needed to speak with him "desperately," that it was "important."

Detective Debbie Regentin was just back from speaking with the Millers at Ann and Eric's West Raleigh home. She had been filling Morgan in on Ann's behavior, how she had locked herself in the bathroom. When Morgan told her about the message from Wang, they both decided not to wait, but instead to race out to Wang's house while her desire to talk was still urgent. They realized she just might have key information that could push the case another step forward. Any step at this point would help. If they waited, Wang might change her mind.

On the way to Wang's house, Morgan recalled his first interview with her; how he'd felt that she was holding back, keeping something from him. He trusted his gut, and now it looked like his gut might be right. This time Wang told Morgan a very different story from the one she'd told at their first meeting.

"She thought something definitely untoward was going on between Ann and Derril," Morgan said. "She told us she and a lot of other people at Glaxo were scared to death because they realized that something was going on."

Wang told Morgan they were scared because of the implications of the affair combined with Eric's death. If the pair had killed one person, could they kill again? She told Morgan about an ongoing fight that Willard and Ann seemed to be having in the lab since Eric's death. She said that when they were around other people, they did not talk to each other. They glared in each other's direction; their icy stares were an indication that something had gone terribly wrong between them. But when everyone else left the work space, Wang told Morgan that she and her colleagues could hear the pair arguing. The exact words were not audible, but Wang told Morgan the fighting went on for hours. Two of the fights had occurred recently—one on January 17, the other on January 19.

Wang also told the detectives that Ann Miller was not the hard worker she had described her as being during their first interview. She told Morgan Ann needed a lot of hand-holding and prodding to get her work done.

" 'She spends more of her day trying to look good for the men she works for and works with than she does actually doing any work,' " Morgan says Wang told him.

Wang also told Morgan she had not been lying the first time, but merely "leaving things out." That since Eric's death everyone in the lab had been concerned about their own safety around the pair whom they thought might actually be murderers. For that reason, Morgan said, they were reticent to share what they knew.

Morgan called Ann's behavior at work after Eric's death

her "postoffense behavior." He said it's a way investigators categorize what people who were close to the victim do after the murder. The behavior may not give them a clue as to who is responsible for the death, but at the very least it can shed some light on who the victim was and what they meant to a particular person.

After a murder, Morgan said, family members experience a range of divergent emotions. Some people become catatonic, others mad, others are humbly able to find peace in sharing positive memories of their loved one. But the one thing they rarely do is act completely normal, which was exactly what Ann Miller did. Nothing.

Morgan often wondered why Ann Miller didn't try to play the I'm-looking-for-my-husband's-killer card. Like O. J. Simpson, or Scott Peterson. He wondered why she didn't bang on the police-station door and demand answers.

"She knows that her husband was killed, that his life was taken, that she and her daughter have been deprived of him for the rest of their lives and she never calls any detective, never wants any information," Morgan says with unparalleled incredulousness in his voice.

"They want to know why aren't you working harder, why aren't more detectives working on this case," Morgan says, recalling what victims' families had said to him over the years. "We never got that from Ann Miller, we got nothing from her, and when you get nothing it makes you wonder why."

In hindsight, Morgan always felt this lack of responsiveness on Ann's part was due to a sense of entitlement, that magical thinking again, a feeling that she was smarter than the police, that she wasn't going to waste her precious time and breath dealing with them, that she was above their little murder investigation. It was a sign, a *telling* sign, to Morgan that investigators were on the right track.

There was one anecdote Wang told Morgan that he couldn't shake. It embodied everything he was learning about Ann and then some. Soon after Eric's death, Wang told Morgan and Regentin, Ann's colleagues, herself included, had taken Ann to a local restaurant for lunch. Wang told Morgan that Ann, who seemed to be in good spirits, ordered a large hamburger and onion rings, which she ate voraciously. This had struck Wang as unusual behavior for a grieving widow. It struck Morgan the same way. He imagined Ann chowing down on a juicy burger and crispy onion rings, delicately dabbing the ketchup on the corners of her mouth with her napkin without a care in the world.

"It confirmed a lot of suspicions I had about Ann Miller," says Morgan.

THE DAY AFTER

As Morgan suspected, the information from the search warrant detailing what was taken from Willard's house was on the front page of the *News and Observer* Monday morning, January 22, 2001.

In addition to listing what was taken from the home, the article talked about how Eric Miller might have received arsenic in his beer at the bowling alley, and highlighted the apparent romantic relationship between Ann Miller and Derril Willard. Not surprisingly, the enterprising reporter, Oren Dorell (who now works for *USA Today*), had connected the dots and pointed the finger as far as he could in the direction of Willard's potential role in Eric's death without actually coming out and saying it.

In Morgan's mind this article would ultimately be the crushing blow, the final straw on Willard's already heavy back. Willard could no longer hide from the fact that he was involved with Ann, and that he might have played a role in Eric's murder. It was on page 1A for the world to see. Derril Willard had run out of time.

FOUR

*Conscience is the inner voice
that warns us someone may be looking.*
—H. L. MENCKEN

Morgan learned about Willard's death in the worst possible way: on the television news. He remembered Jeff Fluck running into his office and excitedly flipping on the five-o'clock local news program. A veteran reporter by the name of Ed Crump, who had worked for the local ABC affiliate for many years, was standing in front of Willard's house doing a live shot, and before Morgan even heard one word come out of his mouth, he *knew*, he knew that his gut had been right about Derril Willard's state of mind.

"It appeared that strange nagging feeling I had had the day before was probably well founded, because it was quickly reported that Derril Willard had been found dead from an apparent self-inflicted gunshot [wound] in his garage," said Morgan, his voice full of regret and remorse.

Willard had been found by his wife, Yvette, and their young daughter when Yvette returned from work. She'd

opened the garage door, and there he was, still in his paja-
mas and slippers. He hadn't even bothered to dress that day,
and why would he? He'd obviously made a decision that
he was going to exit the world, and it didn't matter what he
was wearing.

Crump and his photographer, who were staked out in
front of the Willard house, also got a firsthand glimpse of
the gruesome sight, much to their surprise. They had come
to the house that day simply to follow up on the article in
the newspaper about the search of the home and Willard's
possible connection to Eric Miller's murder. Their goal had
been to interview Willard. When no one answered the door,
they'd waited, assuming that Derril and Yvette were probably at work. When Yvette Willard pulled into the driveway
with her daughter, Kelcey, they moved in closer, hoping to
get her to talk about the case. But as the garage door
opened they were greeted by the horrible sight of Willard's
dead body.

As Ed Crump remembered it, they couldn't make out at
first that there was a body lying on the garage floor. To him
it had simply looked like a pile of couch cushions from the
end of the driveway, as Yvette's car was partially blocking
his view. She immediately closed the garage and went inside. But when the news team went to their live van and replayed their tape, they were horrified to see not sofa
cushions, but the unthinkable, what should have been the
most private of tragedies, caught on tape. Tape that would
never see air, but would be etched in their minds forever.

Morgan admits he hadn't lost too much sleep the night
before the suicide worrying about Willard's fate. In his

mind there was nothing he could have done. His hands were tied. He was the one who'd wanted to arrest Willard on Sunday. Clearly, had Willard been arrested, he would not have been able to kill himself, at least not as easily, in a jail cell. It's a thought that has taken over Morgan's mind more than once in the years since. At the time it bothered him to his core. It sat on Morgan's list of a thousand what-ifs that he would never be able to change. His list was longer than most, and the consequences of the choices made were greater.

But at the time Morgan had other things on his mind. As awful as he felt about the man's death, he couldn't afford to dwell on Derril Willard. "Jeff and his crew sprang into action [to handle the suicide]. I didn't get invited along for the party and didn't feel like there was a whole lot that I could offer," Morgan explains. Since Willard lived in Wake County, not in the Raleigh city limits, the Wake County Sheriff's Office was investigating the suicide.

Also, Morgan was getting ready to head to New York and Boston to interview witnesses in another case, the death of Beth-Ellen Vinson. This was the cold case that concerned a young girl from eastern North Carolina who had come to Raleigh with big dreams, only to have them snuffed out by a killer wielding a knife in a drainage ditch. Morgan had been assigned to reinvestigate the Vinson case, but because of his obsession with the Miller case, his focus had been diverted. It was time for him to get back on track. Unlike the Miller case, the Vinson case was a hundred percent *his* and he was determined to give it his all.

Still Morgan couldn't shake the feeling that he could be,

should be, doing more to help out in the Miller case. He stuck around the office, watched the news reports, and tried to be available in case the investigators working the case needed his help.

The big question, not only for investigators, but for the media, was whether or not Willard had left a suicide note. After all, this wasn't just *any* suicide. It was the suicide of a man intimately connected with a suspect in a murder investigation. If a note had been left, it could possibly provide valuable clues to detectives about Eric Miller's death. Reporters immediately grilled investigators at the scene about whether or not a note had in fact been left. The answer to the question was ultimately yes, Willard did leave a note, but like other key pieces of evidence, Raleigh police felt this was a fact too valuable to release for public consumption just yet.

That night Morgan said Wade Smith, Ann Miller's attorney, called Detective Debbie Regentin and asked her if a note had been left. Clearly, he was concerned that if there *was* a note, it might implicate his client. Morgan says Regentin took the high road and told Smith she wasn't able to give him that information because it was part of an ongoing investigation.

Ultimately, because the suicide wasn't a Raleigh Police Department case, they had no control over the release of information. It was up to the Wake County Sheriff's Office and Major Danny Bellamy. Reporters asked Bellamy about the existence of a note the day after Willard's suicide. Morgan will never forget his answer.

"Danny told the reporters, 'Yeah, we've got a suicide

note, but I don't think anybody is going to be solving any murders from the suicide note that was left by Derril Willard,'" Morgan recalls, appalled. "To this day I still don't know why Danny Bellamy did that."

It was a crushing blow for investigators scrambling to keep important evidence confidential. The more they released, the more the public speculated, and the murkier the water became. In a courtroom, in front of twelve jurors, murky waters equaled reasonable doubt, and in a case like this detectives couldn't afford to leave even a shred of reasonable doubt. In his heart Morgan believes Bellamy simply didn't consider the implications of releasing this information for the murder investigation. After all, he wasn't living and breathing it as members of the Raleigh Police Department were doing.

In Morgan's mind, releasing this information gave Ann Miller and Wade Smith exactly what they wanted—proof that there was nothing in the note to implicate her in her husband's murder. But Morgan wasn't so sure the note was benign.

The note was written in all block capital letters on a single sheet of paper tacked to the garage wall in plain view. Unlike Willard's apparent lack of concern about his appearance, he seemed to have been very concerned that the note be found along with his body. In Morgan's mind Willard had chosen each and every one of his words very carefully, and because of this, they deserved Morgan's equally careful scrutiny. Over the coming years Morgan would read this note over and over, trying to read between the lines, looking for the *real* message that a dead witness was attempting to send from his grave. It was like a code Morgan was forever trying to crack, but without success.

THE NOTE

I AM SORRY TO LEAVE YOU, MY WIFE, MY BEAUTI-FUL DAUGHTER, MY FAMILY AND FRIENDS, LIKE THIS. THE PAST YEAR HAS BEEN FULL OF ANXIETY, SICKNESS AND PAIN. TODAY, I HAVE BEEN AC-CUSED OF AN ACTION FOR WHICH I AM NOT RE-SPONSIBLE. I HAVE TAKEN NO ONE'S LIFE, SAVE MY OWN. THE WORLD LOOKS BLACK TO ME. ALL I CAN SEE IS THE SMEARING OF MY NAME, PAIN CAUSED MY FAMILY, PERSONAL HUMILIATION AND PROBA-BLE ECONOMIC RUIN. I DEEPLY REGRET MY MAN-NER OF LEAVING THE WORLD, BUT HOPE THE [SIC] ANY PAIN CAUSED WILL NOT LINGER—AT LEAST NOT IN THE FASHION THAT MY REMAINING HERE MIGHT ENGENDER. I HAVE BEEN BLESSED WITH A LIFE FULL OF LOVE AND CARING. I LOVE YOU, MY FAMILY. I LOVE YOU, MY DAUGHTER.

I LOVE YOU ALL—

KEEPING SECRETS

Morgan headed to New York undeterred by what appeared to be yet another roadblock in the Miller case—valuable, inside information handed to the defense counsel on a silver platter in the form of the evening news. Again, he had to keep telling himself that it wasn't *his* case. But somehow he knew that if it ever did become his case, these obstacles would come back to haunt him. His gut was right. They did.

While he was driving to New York (because flying was his biggest fear) Morgan got a cell-phone call from Fluck. He wanted to know where the court order form asking a judge to seal an autopsy was located in Morgan's filing cabinet. They wanted to have the details of Eric Miller's autopsy sealed. This would mean that only investigators and prosecutors could have access to the information. No one else, including the victim's family or reporters, could get to it. Morgan had had experience with this issue because Beth-Ellen Vinson's autopsy report had been, and still was, sealed by the original investigators who worked on that case. Immediately, Morgan had a bad feeling that sealing the autopsy was not the correct course of action in the Miller case.

"The more you try and keep a secret that's usually public record, the more apt you are to make everybody suspicious about what's going on," Morgan says. "Sometimes suspicions like that can just derail an investigation."

In Morgan's opinion the Vinson case was a prime example of why not to seal an autopsy report. On one hand, keeping Beth-Ellen's manner of death a secret was a way to root out the person who murdered her. Only her killer would know exactly how she died. This meant that the killer would be more likely to trip himself up during an interview and reveal something about the manner of death that only he or investigators could possibly know. On the other hand, the victim's family members were left totally in the dark about their daughter's manner of death, and as a result, they became suspicious about whether or not detectives were really doing their jobs.

Ultimately, when Vinson's body was sent to the funeral home in Goldsboro, North Carolina, a small, tight-knit community in the eastern part of the state, the truth came out. It was clear from the condition of her body that she had been stabbed multiple times. It became something of a rural legend. Word traveled fast in Wayne County. The secret that investigators and the court had tried so hard to guard was out, despite their best efforts to control the situation.

In the Miller case there was a very different reason for keeping the autopsy report sealed. It was a reason that Morgan to this day can't truly get his mind around. He could not at first for the life of him figure out why in the world Fluck and prosecutor Tom Ford wanted to seal it. It had been clear to him and everyone else involved in the case from the get-go that Eric Miller had been poisoned with arsenic. Morgan couldn't imagine how making the details of the poisoning—which only a scientist could truly decipher—public would hurt the case.

But Morgan says that Fluck and Ford thought that another toxin, something other than arsenic, might also have been involved in Eric Miller's death. Morgan figured they felt that an educated woman like Ann Miller wouldn't *just* use plain old garden-variety arsenic over and over again, that surely she would mix it up a little, add in something else. In Morgan's mind this was, and is to this day, faulty reasoning.

Thankfully no one disagreed at this point that Ann Miller was the most likely suspect in her husband's murder, but they wanted more time to search for the mystery toxin.

Not unlike searching for another suspect in a murder case, looking at a different cause of death can steer you so far away from the truth that it becomes difficult, if not impossible, to get back. No one else shared this opinion about another toxin, including the medical examiner, Dr. Thomas Clark.

"It alienated the medical examiner's office because they didn't see the big mystery here," Morgan says. "The impetus for sealing the autopsy in the Eric Miller case was something that would come to haunt us for years and years."

In Morgan's mind it was a simple case in many ways. On December 4, 2000, during the search of Ann Miller's lab at Glaxo Wellcome, sodium cacodylate, an arsenic compound, had been discovered. Miller and Willard had had easy, unfettered, untraceable access to it. It was more than enough to kill Eric Miller several times over. End of story.

"It's no big mystery, crime makes people stupid, even smart people," Morgan says. "For the great [majority] of murderers who are neither intelligent, nor well educated, it makes them do just ridiculous things."

Fluck had secured his own consultant, pathologist Andy Mason, who was a known expert on arsenic. He was a former employee of the North Carolina Medical Examiner's Office located at the University of North Carolina in Chapel Hill. Morgan was concerned that Mason might share the opinion that another toxin might be involved. The prosecutor had also been talking to Dr. Marsha Ford from the North Carolina Poison Control Office in Charlotte. Morgan said she, too, seemed to have suspicions that there might be another poison involved in Eric's death.

But against Morgan's gut feelings that it should be released, the autopsy was sealed by a judge for three months so that investigators could sort out what some of them saw as a major potential conflict in the evidence. It was a relatively short time compared to some cases, in which the evidence was often sealed indefinitely, as it had been in the Vinson case. For Morgan his concerns were becoming less about the sealing of the autopsy and more about the wild-goose chase that he felt was about to begin as they speculated about a second poison.

MOTIVE OF A MURDERESS

One of the biggest stumbling blocks in the Miller case was figuring out Ann Miller's motive. For the most part Morgan believes motive is usually pretty easy to discern—in short, he believes people generally kill for money or love. But money didn't seem to play a role here, and because Morgan didn't think Ann had the ability to really *love,* that she just toyed with the men in her life, he couldn't imagine her killing for them. As much as she appeared to manipulate, control, and loathe some of the men in her life, why would she kill one man for another?

Morgan admits that as an investigator, you want to pinpoint a motive so badly that you occasionally try to jam a square peg into a round hole and attempt to convince everyone around you that it fits. But motive is not always obvious. In fact, sometimes it's downright elusive. This bothered other investigators more than it did Morgan. For him, having a clear motive wasn't necessary to solve a crime, because he knew that sometimes people just kill. Period.

"It's kind of like peeling away the layers of an onion. It's not something that's readily apparent and readily understandable," Morgan says.

Investigators started peeling the onion. They began looking for something, anything, in Ann Miller's history that might prove she had killed before.

In one interview investigators learned that a man Ann had known had jumped out of a helicopter at a football game and his parachute failed to open. He hit the ground at warp speed and died. *Was Ann responsible?* It seemed implausible, but they were desperate to find something that would give them ammunition, a pattern, a trail of dead bodies.

"There was a kind of fervor to show that Ann had been involved in prior murderess events. Nothing they uncovered actually led to that conclusion," says Morgan.

As far as Morgan was concerned, if a person killed one time, it didn't necessarily mean he or she had killed before, or would ever kill again. It simply meant that a set of circumstances had come together that allowed the person to get away with murder at least once, circumstances that might never have existed before, and might never exist again.

Fluck went back further and further. He interviewed people whom Ann had worked with, people she went to college with at Purdue, people who'd known her in every stage of her life. Sure, not everyone cared for her. There were those who had less than favorable things to say about Ann Miller. She was a "bitch." She was "manipulative." She was a "control freak." She was "unforgivably ambitious." But none of this made her a murderer. It simply made her a person whom others had strong opinions about one way or the other. Chris Morgan knows a little bit about this himself. Morgan is someone whom some people love and some people intensely dislike. Luckily he's also someone who doesn't give a damn which camp you belong to. But he sensed that Ann did care about what people thought of her. This is why, in his mind, she put up such a pretense of being a model wife and mother when in fact she was living on the dark side of humanity.

But Morgan felt investigators needed to cross the motive hurdle in order to move forward. They needed a reason that a well-educated, attractive young woman and mother would take her husband's life in such a gruesome way, allowing him to suffer, and eventually deteriorate into death.

"Nobody ever believed Ann had any designs to live happily ever after with Derril Willard. It was fairly apparent from the very early stages of this case that we all assumed, quite rightly, that Derril Willard was simply a pawn, a tool that was used by Ann Miller," Morgan says with obvious disgust.

Eliminating Willard as a motive left only one other known paramour, Carl Mackewicz. This was the direction in which detectives started to head at this point in the investigation, but it was a dead end to Morgan. Sure, Ann had had an affair with Mackewicz, that much was quite clear. But it didn't seem likely that Carl, or any other *one* man for that matter, was enough for Ann.

As they dug deeper it became obvious that while Eric Miller's past with women was squeaky-clean, Ann Miller's past with men was at the far end of the spectrum—in a word, *wild*. It was commonly known that Eric had "saved" himself for marriage. It was just as commonly known that Ann had not. Apparently, according to some men who had known her in college, Ann was quite experienced in bed. Eric wouldn't have been the first man to succumb to the savvy of a more sexually experienced woman. But Morgan believed Ann's advanced sexual repertoire may have clouded Eric's judgment to the point where he overlooked red flags in the relationship early on, and never saw with complete clarity, even on his deathbed.

DEATH BEHIND BARS

In Morgan's mind the Miller investigation was like a train that had taken so many detours it was amazing that it ever reached its final destination. Every time he thought the train was rushing full-speed ahead toward an arrest, the track split and investigators took what he felt was the wrong path to a distant station. As a result of all the detours, it would take another couple of weeks to get back where they needed to be and begin all over again. It was a never-ending tailspin.

In their desire to connect Ann Miller to another similar death, investigators looked into the lives of every person they could find who had known her. For months their focus settled squarely on her former college roommate at Purdue, Rene Hinson, who seemed to have an intimate knowledge of the *real* Ann, a knowledge that detectives hoped would help them develop leads in the case.

Morgan describes Rene as a goodtime girl who was "attractive enough" and a "big hit with men." After college, Morgan says, Rene was looking for a job when Ann and Eric invited her to come to Raleigh. Rene lived with the newlyweds in their house in Holly Springs for several months as she tried to get her foot in the door somewhere. Ann tried to get her friend work at Glaxo Wellcome, and Eric successfully found her a job at North Carolina State University, where he was working on his doctorate. Rene worked at the University for a short period of time, but nothing permanent materialized for her in North Carolina. Ultimately, she headed home to West Virginia, where she married a man with what Morgan called a "speckled past." Henry Hinson, Rene's husband, was into drugs and weapons, and he ended up doing time in federal prison. As a dutiful wife, Rene visited her husband behind bars, and in August of 2000, after one such visit (accompanied by Henry's grandmother), Henry dropped dead of an apparent heart attack.

But Morgan says the grandmother was not convinced that the death was natural. She went to the West Virginia State Police and told them that Rene had smuggled in a fast-food sandwich to her husband, and that she, the grandmother, was convinced the sandwich contained a poison that killed Henry.

Clearly, this theory intrigued investigators in Raleigh. Two best friends from college whose husbands both died under suspicious circumstances? There *had to be* a connection, or so they assumed. Morgan was not so quick to draw a parallel.

"This caused all sorts of bells and whistles to go off," Morgan says with a chuckle as he recalled the theories. "I would agree on first glance, it's a very strange set of coincidences."

But Morgan didn't think the facts supported this theory. Henry Hinson had a long history of drug use and obvious blockages in his arteries. According to the West Virginia medical examiner, his death was simply the result of a heart attack, case closed.

"Never let the facts get in the way of a good conspiracy," quips Morgan. "There was nothing to connect Henry Hinson's death with poisoning. It's not a question of why did he die, it's a question of why did he live so long with that much blockage in his heart?"

EARL'S GOTTA DIE

Sergeant Jeff Fluck sent detectives Debbie Regentin and Randy Miller to visit Rene Hinson in West Virginia. Once again, Morgan was out of the loop, on the fringes of the investigation. But he hung on every word shared by the detectives when they returned from this particular trip. It was an anecdote that would later add up to little more than a good story, but at the time investigators thought Rene might play an integral role in the case.

Detectives told Morgan that when they entered Hinson's apartment, the song emanating from her CD player was "Earl's Gotta Die," the smash hit by the Grammy-winning country band the Dixie Chicks, about a woman who kills her abusive husband. According to Morgan, this strange coincidence helped sway detectives again toward the theory that Rene had poisoned her husband in prison. Yet Rene denied any involvement in her own husband's death, or for that matter any knowledge of how Eric Miller was killed. Rene said she was friends with both Ann and Eric and didn't believe Ann had anything to do with Eric's death.

But this didn't deter investigators. Morgan says they continued to be sure that Rene was lying as the eerie song, which Rene told them was her "favorite," wafted through the apartment in the background like a funeral dirge.

Morgan eventually got his own crack at Rene Hinson, though by that time, like many other close associates of Ann Miller, she had changed her tune. Too much had been reported at that point about Ann Miller's involvement in Eric Miller's death for Rene to afford to ignore it. Ultimately, no one wanted to be connected with Ann Miller or her actions.

"Initially she was very supportive, but eventually Rene became part of a number of people who wanted to see Ann get what was coming to her," Morgan says smugly.

AUTOPSIES DON'T LIE

But beneath the surface of the slow, plodding pace of the investigation in early 2001, a violent storm was brewing within the Raleigh Police Department. After Eric Miller's autopsy report had been sealed for several months, it was finally time to release it. Even though they knew it was coming, this wasn't sitting well with investigators or the prosecutor. In addition to this development, Morgan felt there was bad blood developing between the medical examiner assigned to the case and the investigative team. As usual, he stepped right into the middle of it.

The battle over whether or not another toxin had been used in Eric's murder created what Morgan termed a "bitter divorce." Assistant District Attorney Tom Ford was still looking for an additional toxin, while the medical examiner, Dr. Thomas Clark, was sure that arsenic alone killed Eric. According to Morgan, the two had exchanged heated letters until eventually communication broke down completely. In general, it's helpful for the medical examiner, investigators, and the prosecutor to form a partnership in a criminal case. Morgan said there was no partnership here—quite the opposite, the relationship was "acrimonious on all parts."

Unfortunately, Morgan wasn't briefed on this background when he was asked to accompany Captain Donald Overman to pick up the autopsy report at the medical examiner's office in Chapel Hill. Their goal was not only to obtain the report, but to get a firsthand briefing from Dr. Clark himself. It was supposed to be a routine meeting, one Morgan had had many times before in other murder investigations, but he had no idea what he was walking into.

"Don Overman and I walked into a storm at the Office of the Chief Medical Examiner of North Carolina," Morgan says, remembering the chilly reception they received.

When Morgan and Overman asked Dr. Clark to walk them through the report, the mood got even colder. But while Morgan agreed that Clark was the doctor and he himself was just a detective, he was a pretty quick study and figured it was Clark's job to give them the report in layman's terms, the same terms that a jury would require. Undaunted, Overman and Morgan insisted on a clear rundown of the report from Clark, and they got it.

Morgan says Clark explained that it looked like Eric had been poisoned the night of November 15, 2000, the night he went bowling with Derril Willard. This presumably happened when Eric drank beer laced with poison, again, presumably given to him by Willard.

The results also appeared to show that Eric had been poisoned *while* he was at Rex Hospital—during his first stay there immediately after the bowling incident. This was determined not just from test results, but from clinical records. They showed that Eric's condition had worsened at Rex and continued to deteriorate in the first few days after being transferred to UNC. How he would have received the arsenic in the hospital was still unclear. In his food? In his water? From whom?

Clark also told detectives that shortly before Eric's second and final hospitalization, he again came in contact with arsenic at home. Investigators theorized that Ann had put the arsenic in Eric's food, which had been prepared by friends from their church.

Clark also explained to the detectives that after analyzing Eric's hair, which allowed for an almost exact footprint of how much arsenic had been received and when, he had been able to determine that Eric had been given many small doses over a period of months.

The amount of arsenic Eric had ingested over the summer hadn't been enough to make him gravely ill, but was enough to keep him out of work, and enough that friends and family had noticed how Eric always seemed to be under the weather. One dose coincided precisely with a July family reunion in Indiana where everyone thought Eric had gotten food poisoning. They were half right, Morgan thought, about the poisoning; but it wasn't rancid potato salad that made him ill: it was *arsenic*.

Morgan and Raleigh Police Department psychologist Dr. Michael Teague continued to wrestle with the issue of the multiple doses throughout the investigation. Clearly,

Ann Miller was smart enough and well versed enough in science to do the math and to figure out how much arsenic would simply make Eric sick, and how much would kill him. The previous small doses had made Eric sick, but the last dose—the deadly dose, the one that investigators thought had been placed in Eric's last meal and fed to him by Ann—actually killed him.

Teague hypothesized to Morgan that perhaps Ann had been punishing Eric with smaller doses of arsenic for not doing what she wanted, for not satisfying her needs, material needs such as a bigger house, a fancier car, and exotic vacations. Morgan, on the other hand, thought Ann might have been experimenting initially, fine-tuning the dosage to see how Eric's body reacted to the poison, to make sure he wasn't immune, or didn't have some sort of unusual tolerance. But eventually, to Morgan's mind, the most likely scenario was that Ann had been giving Eric prior doses in order to create a history of sickness in the months leading up to his death.

He recalled how, during the first and only interview between Ann Miller and Raleigh police, she'd portrayed Eric as sickly, almost as a hypochondriac. Morgan thought this was her way of setting the stage to explain that her husband had died after a long illness, not after someone put a lethal dose of poison in his chicken and rice.

" 'There's where he got poisoned, there's where he got poisoned, there's where he got poisoned, when are you going to arrest her?' " Morgan recalls the doctor saying to him.

Morgan had no good answers for him.

But something good *had* come out of the meeting. In his mind the autopsy was clear—Eric Miller had been poisoned at least three times, and Ann Miller was the most likely suspect on at least two of those occasions. Even if Derril Willard had put arsenic in Eric's beer, he'd likely done so at Ann's bidding, and this ultimately wasn't the dose that killed him. But not everyone saw it Morgan's way, or at least didn't feel his version could be proven beyond a reasonable doubt in a courtroom.

Morgan assumed prosecutors would look at the autopsy report and immediately order the arrest of Ann Miller, but it didn't happen that way; in fact it wouldn't happen for many years to come. Morgan never imagined that in many ways this was just the beginning of his lengthy crusade for justice on Eric Miller's behalf. Like so many long journeys, if he had known in the beginning how rough the trip was going to be, he might never have taken that first step; but also like so many long journeys, the farther you go, the harder it is to turn back. And Chris Morgan was definitely not a person to turn back from anything, especially the truth.

FIVE

Zeal without knowledge is fire without light.
—THOMAS FULLER

Morgan knew Eric Miller's story, or at least the pieces that he felt were important, but to really understand why Eric had died, Morgan also needed to know Ann Miller's story. He needed to know who she was before she met Eric, and who she was while they were together. To Morgan, the couple was living out two very different stories, two very different lives, simultaneously.

Members of the class of 1988 from her high school days in Spring Grove, Pennsylvania, remembered Ann as smart, popular, and pretty—not a girl anyone would have pegged as a future murderer. Future scientist, future wife, and future mother, maybe, but definitely not a future killer.

But Morgan always viewed this "perfect" facade as the window dressing that hid Ann's psychopathic tendencies. As he saw it, it was something she had perfected throughout her adult life, the ability to appear one way on the outside, but to be something totally different on the inside.

"She wasn't remorseful, she wasn't scared, she was just what she was: confident, cool, collected," Morgan said.

Psychopathy is often incorrectly confused with psychosis, but in reality psychopathy is not an official medical or mental condition. According to the dictionary, it is derived from the Greek words *psyche,* which means "soul," and *pathos,* which means "to suffer."

The American Psychiatric Association believes that psychopathy is an outdated word used to describe someone who suffers from antisocial personality disorder. These people lack empathy, are highly manipulative, and cannot control their impulses. In short, they lack a conscience. Because people with these traits are often high functioning and very successful in today's competitive world, they are not always recognized by our society as being deviant.

Former Raleigh Police Department psychologist Dr. Michael Teague saw these behavioral traits as fitting in perfectly with his theory of magical thinking. The way Teague saw it, in her mind Ann could do no wrong. She was quick to blame others for her problems and her transgressions. Because psychopaths have no real concern for others, the only way that they function in society is by mimicking what they know is considered acceptable behavior. Teague felt this described Ann Miller exactly. He was careful to point out, though, that someone who is psychopathic is not mentally ill in the traditional sense—that such a person is still totally competent, aware of, and legally responsible for her actions.

People who knew Ann and Eric saw their differences, but still didn't question the image of the loving couple they portrayed to the world. Ann and Eric were active members of their Catholic church in Raleigh, even leading marriage workshops and organizing retreats for other young couples. But despite their appearing as role models of a good marriage, trouble was already brewing in paradise, even if Eric didn't know it at the time.

Morgan says Ann met Carl Mackewicz on January 17, 1997, exactly three years to the day before she would give birth to her daughter, Clare, at Rex Hospital. Throughout those three years Ann saw Carl Mackewicz often, e-mailed back and forth with him, and called him frequently.

Investigators uncovered evidence that the two met in San Francisco, where Mackewicz lived. They also discovered that the pair had taken romantic jaunts to places like Lake Tahoe, New York, and the Outer Banks of North Carolina. But apparently Eric had been oblivious to the relationship, or if he was aware of it, he didn't know it was sexual. Ann had portrayed it to others as a work friendship, nothing more.

Ann received an in vitro fertilization treatment on April 20, 1999. Soon after the fertility treatment, unbeknownst to Eric, Morgan said Ann spent five days with Mackewicz on the North Carolina coast. On May 8, 2000, she sent the following e-mail to Carl remembering their trip from the previous year:

> *What a year it's been. Sometimes it seems just like yesterday that we were walking along the Carolina shoreline*

searching for crab shell, sitting under the moonlight
sipping daiquiris . . .

When Ann and Eric's daughter, Clare, was born on January 17, 2000, Ann should have been elated. She had finally gotten what she claimed she'd wanted. For most women the birth of their first child is the beginning of something beautiful and quite unlike anything they've experienced before. But for Ann, Morgan believed her foray into motherhood may have been one of the things that pushed her past the edge of reason. After all, putting someone else's needs before her own was not her forte. In addition, having a baby usurp her spot as the center of attention in her home would not have been palatable to a woman who craved the spotlight.

Dr. Teague strongly believes that Ann may also have suffered from postpartum depression. She would often leave the baby in Eric's capable hands so that she could have some time to herself. Part postpartum depression, part egocentricity, was Teague's professional assessment. He described Ann as a woman who possessed a "toxic level of narcissism."

For Morgan, *understanding* Ann Miller was never his goal. Honestly, he didn't want to get that close to the woman. He simply wanted to find something that would give her away, something that would give investigators the evidence they needed to arrest her. But it was hard to learn more about Ann, or her behavior, because in the spring of 2001, she moved out of the Raleigh area, away from the watchful eyes of investigators.

Ann left her job at Glaxo Wellcome after Derril
Willard's suicide and moved to Wilmington, a coastal city
in North Carolina about two hours east of Raleigh. It was
assumed that she went to Wilmington because her younger
sister Danielle lived there with her husband and children.
Initially, Ann and Clare stayed with Danielle's family, then
in April 2001, Ann rented her own home.

It wasn't as if she'd moved to Mexico, but Ann was just
far enough away to be out of the Raleigh detectives' easy
reach. This frustrated Morgan to no end. Little did he know
he would soon get his chance to be her shadow.

TURNING UP THE HEAT

Despite the damning autopsy report that seemed to point
directly at Ann Miller, it was clear to Morgan that Assistant
District Attorney Tom Ford was still not going to authorize
her arrest.

"Tom, I think, over the years sort of got gun-shy," Morgan theorizes.

Morgan and Ford had originally come to Raleigh around
the same time. But while Morgan grew more passionate
about his work over the years, he felt that Ford had gone
in the opposite direction. For many people the district attorney's office is a stepping-stone to bigger things, but for
Ford it had become a career ender, a place where he was
the top dog and enjoyed a certain amount of power and
freedom.

Morgan decided it was time for him to do whatever he

could to nudge Ford in the right direction. With Sergeant Jeff Fluck and Lieutenant Gerald Britt out of town again, he felt it was up to him to take the ball and run with it. He started trying to figure out what had, and had not, been done in the investigation. One of the first big problems he uncovered was the existence of a great big file cabinet full of information that had never been transmitted to the district attorney's office. While Sergeant Fluck had been keeping Tom Ford updated via phone calls, Ford had not yet actually seen a single document from the reports that investigators had been compiling for months.

Morgan immediately asked Detective Hervoline Faulkner to spend every waking moment making a copy of the files for Ford. The entire case was organized neatly into binders and sent over to the district attorney's office.

"Naturally, Tom Ford was chuckling on the sidelines because he knew he had the perfect out," Morgan recalls. Morgan knew that Ford could simply say he wasn't ready to make an arrest because he had only just received this voluminous file—and he'd have a point.

The next thing Morgan realized was that a time line was missing from the investigation, a chronological history of events from the case put down on paper for everyone to see and refer to, including events leading up to, surrounding, and following Eric Miller's murder. Nothing was too insignificant to include.

So Morgan and lead detectives Randy Miller and Debbie Regentin sat down and created it, in the belief that it was critical to any complex criminal investigation. Their situation could be compared to that overwhelming feeling you

1076382553

have when you dump out a five-hundred-piece jigsaw puzzle on your kitchen table and try to imagine how you could ever possibly assemble it, but somehow you do it. Morgan started with the edges of the Ann Miller puzzle and worked his way into the center until he started to see the image that he was looking for. Without this kind of organization, he could never hope to put the pieces of the puzzle together in a coherent manner.

Since Morgan had been kept out of the loop for so many months, he wanted to pick the brains of all of the investigators who'd worked on the case to see what they knew and what they still needed to find out. Creating a time line was the perfect way for him to fill in the gaps.

One of the things that Morgan discovered from these discussions was that no one had yet asked for the visitors' logs from Rex Hospital and UNC Hospitals. Because Dr. Thomas Clark was convinced that Eric Miller had been poisoned during his first hospital stay at Rex, getting this information was critical.

As it turned out, that very same day a news crew from the local ABC station had asked Rex Hospital for the very same logs. Hospital administrators denied them access to the information, but Morgan was embarrassed that it had taken so long for his team to make the same request that the media made.

At last, the team was making progress, in part thanks to Morgan's pressure to do whatever they could to make their case a stronger one. It was time to lay their cards on the table. Morgan went first and told his colleagues how far he thought they had come and where he felt the investigation needed to go next.

"I don't think Ford can stall too long," Morgan recalls saying. "I think we've got ample probable cause to make an arrest. And I think we should plan within the next couple of weeks on making that arrest so we can bring this thing to an end."

Morgan will never forget what came next. As usual he spoke without censoring himself, or thinking about what he was going to say. This had become a distinct pattern in his life, and one that at his age wasn't likely to change.

"I would later come to regret opening my big mouth once again," Morgan rues, "as I have so often over the years."

It was May 2001—a full six months after Eric Miller's murder. Morgan told his colleagues that they really didn't know anything about Ann Miller's life *now*. They knew she had moved to Wilmington to be closer to her family, and it made total sense for Ann to go where her support system was. But that's about all they knew. They didn't know where she worked, or whom she was spending time with. Morgan pointed out that maybe after getting out of Raleigh, where she had been watched, Ann would feel safer, safe enough to talk to someone and maybe tell him or her something about the case. Out loud, Morgan speculated that just maybe, if that someone did exist, he or she might be willing to talk to police.

"If this were my case, I would have her on round-the-clock surveillance," Morgan said vigorously to the group of assembled investigators.

No sooner had the words escaped his lips than Morgan realized exactly what he was in for. If he was eager to tail Ann Miller, then the Raleigh Police Department would grant his wish.

" 'Since you've got such a brilliant idea there, pack your bags, you're moving to Wilmington,' " says Morgan, remembering the day his bosses gave him his marching orders.

PRIVATE EYES WATCHING YOU

"It was an interesting case, she was an interesting woman, and I felt like it was something that was important," Morgan insists, trying to put his assignment in the best light possible.

Morgan rounded up a team of half a dozen or so detectives. As luck would have it, the stepmother of one of his detectives lived on the very street in Wilmington where Ann Miller had rented a house. This gave them a way to begin their undercover surveillance without being noticed.

In May 2001, the team checked in to the Comfort Inn in Wilmington, donned their Bermuda shorts and golf shirts, and started watching Ann Miller's every move.

"It's kind of creepy because you're actually *trying* to watch people, I mean there's a tinge of voyeurism in it," Morgan says unapologetically.

Investigators discovered that Ann was working at an interior-design store near Wrightsville Beach, a resort community just outside of Wilmington. Her routine was fairly consistent. She would drop Clare at her sister Danielle's house in the morning, go to work, pick Clare up in the afternoon, and then return to her rental home.

"Her appearance was far from someone who was devastated," Morgan scoffs. "She was in control, she was upbeat, and she carried herself with an air of confidence . . . She wasn't what I expected. She wasn't someone who was fearful, somebody who was scared, or somebody who was anxious, or somebody who was depressed. She was just somebody who was going about business and doing her everyday thing. Outwardly, at least, without a care in the world."

At this point the public speculation had clearly tilted toward Ann being responsible for Eric's death. While the police hadn't actually come out and said this, they danced around the issue in the media just enough to make everyone aware that Ann was the focus of the investigation. Given this, Morgan thought it was unconscionable that Ann could walk around as if nothing were going on. In his mind this was just more proof of her "psychopathic personality."

Morgan recalls that one of the hardest aspects about following Ann Miller was her "chameleon car." She had traded in her big-payment Chevy Suburban for a more modest used Acura Integra. It was a strange color that in some lights looked blue, and in others black or purple, which made the car hard to follow and easy to lose.

Investigators quickly noticed that Ann had a male friend who was hanging around and visiting her house in the evenings. He lived in her sister Danielle's subdivision and seemed to be friendly with the entire family. It immediately piqued Morgan's interest that Ann would be entertaining a gentleman friend so soon after her husband's death.

Investigators learned that the mystery man was named Paul Kontz. Kontz had been born in October 1961 in Queens, New York, to Henry and Patricia Kontz. Unlike Ann, he had no advanced degrees, not even a college degree. He was a sometime electrician and a sometime musician in a Christian rock band.

To Morgan the relationship between the two *appeared* to be romantic, based on the amount of time they were spending together, but since they had not made any public displays of affection in front of the cops, the theory was still up in the air. But if it was in fact a budding romance, it would raise a huge red flag for Morgan. For almost anyone suffering through the loss of a spouse, it would have been too soon. Six months, Morgan thought, was clearly not enough time to get over your husband's murder and jump into someone else's bed. But Ann Miller was not most people.

"People like Ann Miller have no remorse. It's evident in her behavior every day. It's evident to this day. She doesn't feel sorry for what she did. She's not even sorry that Eric's dead, and I think that was one of the first tip-offs," Morgan states definitively.

Morgan thought about cops he knew who, for example, had been involved in a completely justified suspect shooting, yet who had trouble sleeping at night for many years. He thought about what he calls "chicken-leg murders" where two people get into a confrontation fueled by alcohol at the dinner table, and one person ends up killing the other. In those situations, Morgan says, the killers almost always called 911 because the guilt was unbearable to their conscience. But not Ann Miller, no; she was the exception to almost every rule Morgan had learned to trust and rely upon over his years as an investigator. In her world rules didn't seem to apply.

A MOTHER'S LOVE

Yet another red flag to Morgan was Ann's relationship with her by then one-and-a-half-year-old daughter, Clare. One of Morgan's detectives noticed repeatedly that while Ann was never mean or physically abusive to the child, she was also not outwardly loving or nurturing with her. This struck Morgan as particularly odd because he assumed that in a normal situation where a woman had lost her husband, she would be even more likely to cling to the child and smother her with love.

On one occasion, Ann took a stroll on the campus at the University of North Carolina in Wilmington with Paul Kontz. Detectives watching her used a video camera to document the encounter. Ann's once mousy-brown hair was now in a chic, fully highlighted strawberry-blond pixie cut, and her loose-fitting tan pants, sneakers, and fashionable department-store tie-dyed shirt made her look as carefree as any college student walking across the campus.

Ann and Paul strolled and chatted along a tree-lined

sidewalk while Clare (in a pink dress, leggings, and white sandals) played nearby. But unlike most doting first-time mothers, Ann seemed hardly to notice her seventeen-month-old daughter. In fact, she barely acknowledged the child's presence. Ann's smiles and laughs were reserved for Kontz, not her daughter. Kontz actually interacted with the child more than Ann did, picking Clare up in the parking lot on the way to the car, swinging her up into the air, turning her upside down until she giggled.

The most telling moment for Morgan came as Ann went to put her daughter into the backseat of the car. Instead of pulling the child to her chest to protect her tiny head as she leaned into the car, Ann held Clare several inches away from her as if she were holding a dirty diaper and then slung her into the backseat of the car like a bag of groceries.

In Morgan's mind Ann's apparent lack of feelings about her beautiful child once again reinforced what he thought of her—that she was a woman who was capable of loving no one but *herself*.

DIGGING DEEPER

"In the second week of surveillance we got a little bit of a shock," Morgan recalls. Detectives had been sure that they were the only people following Ann Miller, but it turned out that this wasn't the case at all.

Investigators were trading out cars and regrouping at

nearby Ogden Elementary School, when they saw an NBC affiliate's news van from Raleigh driving through the parking lot. Luckily, the news crew didn't appear to notice the detectives. But the next day, as Morgan was pulling down Ann's street to begin his evening stakeout, he noticed a black SUV parked in *his* usual, low-key spot. Unlike a real investigator, the driver of the car was chatting with someone in the backseat and occasionally picking up a pair of binoculars. Morgan knew right away they had to be members of the media. And as soon as Ann pulled into her driveway, a news crew jumped out of the SUV and approached her, microphone and camera in hand. Morgan sat back in the anonymous comfort of his undercover car and watched the circus unfold.

Ultimately, the TV news got nothing but Ann's picture and a terse "no comment," but still ran an exclusive story that night touting the fact they that knew where Ann Miller was now living.

"We were all getting tired of following Ann. We were getting tired of sleeping in a motel, decided that probably we needed to dig a little bit deeper, and that was the night we stole Ann's garbage," Morgan says.

Morgan is quick to point out that it is actually legal to search a person's garbage; once something is put out on the street to be picked up, any expectations of privacy are forfeited.

Not unlike events in an episode of *C.S.I.,* investigators drove quietly into Ann's neighborhood under the cloak of darkness around 2 a.m. Prior to their arrival, they spent an hour disconnecting all of the interior lights in their rented Ford Expedition so that when they opened the door to grab the garbage no one would be able to see inside of the car. They never stopped the vehicle, just rolled by the house at a low speed, reached out, scooped up the bag, and dragged it into the back of the car. But unlike *C.S.I.,* where the forensic team would go through the garbage in a lab with their rubber gloves, for the next few hours detectives used their bare hands to pick through dirty diapers and junk mail on the ground next to the Dumpster at the hotel.

Also unlike *C.S.I.,* they found nothing useful in Ann's garbage—no shredded love notes, no documents about arsenic, no photographs of her and other men. About the only interesting thing at all was a letter that had been torn in half, presumably by Ann herself, from the *News and Observer* reporter Oren Dorell, requesting an interview—the same reporter who had broken the story about the search of Willard's home. Dorell had obviously discovered Ann's new address, maybe even before the cops did. He was that good.

With the garbage just another dead end, investigators went back to simply watching Ann, hoping that she would give something away in a moment of weakness, something they might be able to use against her.

"Most of the time Ann was a very cool customer, she was very relaxed, she was very at ease with herself and her surroundings—which for somebody, once again, whose husband had just been murdered in such a horrible way, such a short time ago . . . I mean it just struck me as peculiar," emphasizes Morgan.

AUTOPSY GOES PUBLIC

While Morgan was watching Ann Miller in Wilmington, the official autopsy report went public in Raleigh. Morgan and Don Overman had received about a five-day advance notice of the release from Dr. Thomas Clark. But now it was out in the media, up for public consumption and public scrutiny.

Morgan had gotten up early that morning and picked up the first copy of Raleigh's hometown newspaper, the *News and Observer,* which made its way slowly to the coastal town. He was eager to see how the results of the autopsy were being spun in print. At the same time he was preparing for another long day of watching Ann Miller. But he assumed this day would be different; on this day Ann Miller would finally know what investigators knew, that Eric Miller had been given several doses of arsenic before his death. Not only that, she would know that everyone else in North Carolina knew it, too.

Despite the release of the report, however, the day seemed like any other for Ann. She went to work on time, got home on time, and appeared to be acting normally. Late afternoon, around four, Morgan parked in Ann's sister Danielle Wilson's neighborhood to watch as Ann picked up Clare. There was one spot where he could sit and get a partial view of the Wilsons' backyard and patio. Ann was in the habit of coming in through the back door, picking up Clare, and then walking her through the house and coming out the front door. Leaning back in his seat, fighting boredom, discomfort, and extreme fatigue, Morgan watched as Ann moved down the walk to the Wilsons' home. Suddenly he sat up straight and grabbed the wheel, leaning closer to the windshield to get a good look. He noticed that Ann seemed to be *marching* toward the door in a very determined manner. Something had changed.

He saw that she was on the phone having a very animated conversation. It was the first time Morgan had seen Ann agitated. Adrenaline moved through his body like a double shot of espresso, his heart started beating faster as he leaned in to his windshield to get a closer look. Ann's neatly pressed tan slacks and simple long-sleeved black sweater gave her a conservative, almost innocent appearance, which contrasted sharply with her wild demeanor.

"She was almost stomping around, stomping her feet. It was obvious that she was very upset about something. To this day I don't know who she was talking to, but I've always felt in my own mind she was probably talking to one of her lawyers because the autopsy report made it look very, very bad for Ann," Morgan recalls with a tinge of childlike glee in his voice.

Morgan felt like the complexity of the autopsy report had been simplified enough in the newspaper to give the impression to the general public that Ann was the most likely suspect in her husband's murder. As Morgan points out, you didn't need to be a scientist to understand the logic that whoever had killed Eric Miller had probably given him all, or most, of the doses of arsenic, and that person had to be someone who was close to the victim.

"She was shaking her fist while she was talking," Morgan says. "She was enraged. She was animated. To be honest with you, that was probably the most emotion I've ever seen come out of Ann Miller."

IN THE BUSH

"I like to always remember it as the day I spent in the oleander bush," says Morgan of his last day in Wilmington.

It was the one day that Ann deviated from her routine, something any good investigator knows is an important clue. When people who usually follow a consistent pattern change it, something fishy is probably going on.

Ann dropped Clare off at the usual time at her sister's house. Nothing out of the ordinary; she appeared to be dressed for work. But then, instead of heading out of the subdivision on her way to the office, she turned in to Paul Kontz's driveway. From what Morgan knew about Ann Miller by this point, it was clear she didn't have very many male friends who didn't eventually turn into lovers. Morgan felt strongly that this was the day when investigators might find proof that Paul Kontz had graduated from friendship to Ann Miller's bed. So Morgan posted up in the only cover he could find outside Kontz's home—an oleander bush. And he waited, and waited, and waited.

"Is it being nosy? Yes. I plead guilty, but I needed to know," Morgan says, half sounding like he's trying to convince himself of this fact.

The blinds were closed, the doors shut, and no one could

be seen moving about the house. Morgan remembers sitting in that "damn bush" for eight hours or more. It was hot, uncomfortable, and endlessly boring. Very few people could sit in a scratchy bush on a warm spring day and *not* be uncomfortable, but for a man of Morgan's stature, there was really no way to make it better. He was also getting eaten alive by mosquitoes. The only thing he had for entertainment was his handheld police radio. He listened to his fellow detectives banter back and forth about the stakeout as they speculated what might be taking place inside the house.

"When detectives get really bored, their minds usually go like most other people's minds: they think dirty thoughts, and this case was no exception," says Morgan with a chuckle.

Morgan was relieved when Ann finally left the house because it meant he could finally get out of the bush. She left alone, just in time to act as if she'd come from work, and went back to her sister's house to pick up Clare.

To Morgan, Ann's impassive face showed no signs of what had taken place inside. A marathon sex session? Tearful confessions about killing her husband? Who knew. But either way Morgan was convinced that Paul Kontz was heading down a very dangerous path, right into the clutches of a woman who would no doubt control him as she had all the others.

The stakeout was over. They had learned everything they were going to learn by watching Ann. Captain Don Overman summoned the team back to Raleigh. It was time to lay the entire case on the table, and see who was brave enough to take it on.

POINTING FINGERS

When Morgan returned from Wilmington, he saw that things had gotten worse between the medical examiner, Dr. Thomas Clark, and the prosecutor, Tom Ford.

"This was something that, in my experience, was unheard of," Morgan says of the ongoing feud.

There was even talk from Ford of filing formal charges against Clark for hindering the investigation says Morgan. Although it ultimately never happened, this kind of talk was something completely unorthodox in Morgan's experience with criminal investigations.

"I had known this case was in trouble for months, but I didn't realize *how much* trouble it was in until that point," he says, shaking his head.

Amid the heat of this battle, Eric Miller's family was eager to find out what was going on with the investigation on the heels of the autopsy results. In the summer of 2001, they were invited to come once again to Raleigh and be briefed on the status of the case. Eric's parents, Doris and Verus Miller, came from Indiana, and his sisters, Pam Baltzell of Kentucky, and Leeann Magee of Pennsylvania, also attended the meeting.

Morgan was invited to come to the meeting because of his recent surveillance of Ann, and to share whatever information they found, or as it turned out, had not found.

"I told them, 'She's not looking over her shoulder, she's not worried about anything, she's not worried about someone coming to kill her and her daughter, guess why?

Because she killed her husband,'" Morgan says, matter-of-factly recalling his words to them.

As expected, Ford told the family he had just received the paperwork from investigators and had not had time to review it. This was a no-win situation for investigators, because this time Ford was right. Morgan had been the one who had pushed to get the case file copied and sent to Ford, but it was so voluminous there was no way Ford could possibly have pored through and digested the whole thing by this time.

Ford and Morgan could not have been more different. The prosecutor was a slight, studious-looking man with wire-framed glasses and long blond hair brushed back behind his ears. In the seventies he might have been the laid-back hippie type, but now he was the lawyer sitting across the table and holding all of the power in his hands.

What happened next turned Morgan's stomach in a way that he will never forget.

"Tom Ford took a very adversarial stance with the Millers. It was almost like he treated the Millers as a suspect's family as opposed to the victim's family. He said, 'We've got to do a little further examination of Eric's life, nobody's this clean and good,'" Morgan says, recalling the gist of Ford's words. "And to this day I don't think I've ever heard anybody say anything quite so outrageous. It was just a reprehensible [approach] for anybody to take face-to-face with the victim's family."

After the autopsy report was released, the Millers had expected that something was going to happen soon. They'd hoped that something would be the arrest of the person responsible for Eric's murder. They did not expect to get beaten up like this.

Morgan recalls Ford also lamenting about how much work it was going to take to get the case ready for trial, that it would take him away from his family, and that it would not be worth it for a case he wasn't sure he could win.

"I was almost dumfounded by what he says at that particular moment," Morgan seethes, not hiding his disgust. "I tried to pretend that I didn't hear it. I think that most of the law enforcement people all around the table all want to pretend that we didn't hear it because it just sounded awful. I mean, there's no way to defend that. It was like saying your son, your brother, isn't worth a year of my time unless I've got an ironclad case that I know can't lose."

Thinking back on his own career, Morgan can't even count the number of birthdays, holidays, and other family events that took place without him because he was working at the police department. And during those times he never knew if what he was doing would contribute to the ultimate success of a case, or if it would be a wasted effort that meant another Thanksgiving dinner missed, another child's birthday party unattended, another Christmas Eve without Dad for no good reason.

All of the detectives, including Morgan, had worked furiously on the Miller case, and they had all given up precious moments in their personal lives to pursue justice for Eric.

"It was a slap in the face to all of us. And it was a slap

directly in the face of the Millers," Morgan says bitterly. "I saw a look come over Verus Miller's face that I will never forget. I mean it was just pure rage."

From what he'd learned about Eric's father, Verus Miller, Morgan knew he was a man who'd worked hard all of his life to provide for his family, *even* if it meant missing things that he really wanted to do. He was not a man who would easily understand an unwillingness to work as hard as possible, especially not by someone in a position of authority, someone like a prosecutor on his son's homicide case.

The Millers would remember Ford's comments for years to come, often bringing them up to Morgan as a turning point in their view of the case. After hearing the prosecutor's perspective, they realized that there might be no justice for their son after all. It was then that Morgan decided *he* would spend every ounce of energy he had, every waking hour, pursuing justice for Eric if that's what it took to solve this case and restore this family's dignity.

"It was a tough, tough situation. And it was even going to get tougher before we were done," Morgan says.

MOVING UP, MOVING OUT

For cops, moving up in rank often means moving out of the unit where they have been working and trying something new. The Raleigh Police Department was no exception to how the law enforcement career ladder functions.

For years Morgan had refused to throw his hat into the

ring for a promotion to lieutenant. Truth was, he never even tried, never even filed the paperwork. He liked his job in homicide. He didn't want to move on, not yet, maybe never.

"There has to be an advocate, there has to be somebody looking out for the dead. They can't speak for themselves and their families often are ill equipped and unable to speak effectively for them," Morgan says.

But this time around the pressure was too great. The interim chief, John Knox, had made it clear to Morgan that he was leaving homicide whether he became a lieutenant or not. Morgan said Knox told him he was a natural leader and he needed him to lead the police department in another area. So like a good soldier, in the fall of 2001, Morgan put in his paperwork for the promotion, anticipating leaving homicide.

Around the same time, in September of 2001, the city of Raleigh hired a new police chief, a woman named Jane Perlov from New York City. The shock around the department was twofold: not only was she a woman, but like the mocking salsa ads, the word around the station when they heard the news was, *New York City?*

The first time Morgan met Perlov he was on the phone with a reporter from the *Goldsboro News Argus* talking about the Beth-Ellen Vinson murder, another one of his cold-case obsessions. He covered the receiver just long enough to say a polite hello and then continued with his call. After all, he was a busy man, one who couldn't be bothered with chitchat and pleasantries when there were murders to be solved. This brief meeting would foreshadow the relationship between Morgan and his boss for the next several years.

"Turned out that Perlov and I would have a stormy, to say the least, relationship," Morgan says with a certain fondness as he recalls their professional sparring.

Soon after Perlov arrived the 9/11 terrorist attacks happened on the World Trade Center in New York. Morgan remembers it as an incredibly unsettled time for everyone in law enforcement, especially their new leader, who had many friends directly affected by the violence. For a time, albeit a short time, Ann Miller did not take center stage in anyone's life. She had been kicked to the curb by a much greater threat: terrorism.

"There was a terrorist under every rock and a new threat every time you turned around," Morgan says with exhaustion in his tone.

But Morgan had his first real run-in with Perlov as soon as the aftershocks of 9/11 subsided in Raleigh. It was the first of many times when the two strong personalities would bump heads.

Oren Dorell, the *Raleigh News and Observer* reporter, had written an article that week quoting Morgan about creating a cold-case squad on the police force. It detailed how Morgan thought it would be beneficial to dedicate focused resources specifically to unsolved murders. Morgan claims the quotes were actually taken from an interview he'd done with the reporter earlier in the year, *way* before Perlov took over. Nonetheless, as soon as the article appeared, Morgan was summoned to Perlov's office.

"I think her intention was to chew my ass . . . she

thought I was undercutting her," Morgan says like a kid who's been sent to the principal's office for the first time.

Morgan told Perlov that he couldn't possibly inform her about every case he was working on, or about every interview he did with a reporter. He also told her that he thought they did need a cold-case unit. At the time they had seventeen unsolved homicides dating back to the unsolved shooting death of hotel clerk Clyde Sykes in 1981 (eventually solved with DNA in June 2007). Not a lot compared to most cities, but these cases were not getting attention as long as new ones kept coming in. Morgan felt that *every* victim deserved his attention.

According to Morgan, "She viewed it as a personal attack; this would set the tone for my interaction with her over the next three or four years."

Despite his rough start with the new chief, however, Morgan was still somehow miraculously promoted to lieutenant *and* permitted to stay in homicide. This was the break he had been waiting for, not just in his career, but in the Ann Miller case. All homicide cases now fell under his jurisdiction. Now he finally had the power to push the Miller investigation in the direction he saw fit. His first order of business was to get the keys to the filing cabinet so that he could read every last piece of paper that had anything to do with the case.

"Nobody was going to exclude me anymore," Morgan says triumphantly.

SIX

A hunch is creativity
trying to tell you something.
—FRANK CAPRA

Even though he finally had the keys to the kingdom—
unfettered access to all of the files in the Eric Miller case—
it would still be weeks before Chris Morgan had a chance
to read them. With his new promotion came new duties.
Around this time another murder case fell into his lap. A
ninety-one-year-old woman named Beulah Dickerson had
been murdered in her home, beaten to death in an apparent
robbery attempt. It irked Morgan to no end that someone
could take the life of an elderly woman and just simply
walk away, free as a bird, unscathed, unconcerned. Frankly,
it irked him that *anyone* could take *anyone's* life, but when
it came to older people, he had a soft spot in his heart the
size of Texas.

For now the Miller case would have to take a backseat.
There were too many pressing issues at hand. The Dickerson
case was weighing heavily on his mind and his shoulders.

Morgan believed that a young woman from the neighborhood had killed Dickerson with a tire iron that had been discovered in a bush near the home. The motive—plain old robbery. The clincher was that the tire iron they'd found was specific to a very small number of General Motors cars made between 1978 and 1979, and the neighbor, they discovered, drove one of those models. Unfortunately, this alone was not enough to charge the young woman, and Morgan's gut feelings about the case were definitely not enough to get the D.A. to okay an arrest.

"The most frustrating cases that I've ever had to deal with were always cases where you knew who was responsible, but you weren't able to put a case together sufficiently to eliminate reasonable doubt," says Morgan, traveling a road in his mind he'd gone down many times before.

Even with efforts to keep everything separate, Morgan began to see parallels between Beulah Dickerson and Eric Miller. They were two very different people from two very different worlds, but they had one very important thing in common: they left a trail of loved ones in their wake who needed answers. And at this point Morgan felt he was one of the few people in a position to provide those answers if he only worked hard enough.

"I kept thinking about how tragic it was, when tragic things like this happen to good, decent people. With every victim there is always a secondary group of victims—their family, their friends, their loved ones," Morgan explains. "Eric Miller was the paradigm case . . . a man who had had a profound impact on everybody he had touched through his life."

In November of 2001, the police department held its official grandiose promotion ceremony at the BTI Center, the city's performing-arts facility. Morgan was finally going to be crowned a lieutenant after years of resisting the change. Dickerson's family attended to show their gratitude for the hard work Morgan had done on the case, despite not being able to make an arrest. It was almost too much pressure for Morgan to take—looking out into the audience, seeing the desperate family, a family not unlike the Millers, yearning for truth and justice. It made his promotion bittersweet; it made him wonder if he really deserved it when he could not solve the murders that constantly screamed out for his attention. It made him *doubt,* a feeling that had always been Morgan's biggest enemy.

In the weeks following his promotion, Morgan was overwhelmed with his new role as a lieutenant in the Homicide Division. For the first time in his career, he had a paper trail to follow and keep up with. Morgan was a talker, not a note taker; he was a shoot-from-the-hip kind of guy, not a pencil pusher. Day after day he sat at his desk thinking, *This is not why I became a cop, to do this, to sit here while everyone else is out on the street preventing and solving crimes.*

"The fears that I had always had about being a lieutenant were instantly realized. I was deluged with paperwork and with jobs that had absolutely nothing to do with putting bad people in jail," Morgan says with resignation.

At the same time Morgan was also overwhelmed by the need to solve the Dickerson case. Detectives finally brought

Eric Miller and baby daughter, Clare, summer 2000
(Courtesy of Verus L. Miller)

Eric Miller celebrates Halloween, October 2000
(Courtesy of Verus L. Miller)

AMF Bowling Lanes, Raleigh, North Carolina
(Chad Flowers)

Derril Willard
(Courtesy of WRAL News)

Derril and Yvette
Willard's house,
Raleigh, North Carolina
(Chad Flowers)

Ann Miller is arrested, September 27, 2004
(The Raleigh News & Observer)

Rex Hospital (where Eric Miller died, December 2, 2000)
(Chad Flowers)

Colon Willloughby,
Wake County
District Attorney
*(Courtesy of Wake County
DA's Office)*

Rebecca Holt,
Wake County
Assistant District Attorney
(Courtesy of WRAL News)

WAKE COUNTY COURTHOUSE

Wake County
Courthouse
(Chad Flowers)

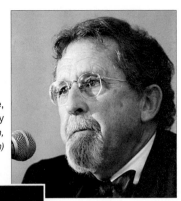

Joseph Cheshire,
Ann Miller's attorney
*(Courtesy of Nathan Clendenin,
WRAL.com)*

Rick Gammon, Derril
Willard's attorney
(Courtesy of WRAL News)

Wade Smith,
Ann Miller's attorney
*(Courtesy of Nathan Clendenin,
WRAL.com))*

Ann Miller pleads guilty, November 7, 2005
(The Raleigh News & Observer)

Paul Kontz, Ann Miller's second husband
(Courtesy of WRAL News)

William Christopher Morgan, homicide investigator
(Courtesy of William Christopher Morgan)

Judge Donald Stephens,
Wake County Chief Resident Superior Court Judge
(Chad Flowers)

Verus and Doris Miller, Eric Miller's parents
(Courtesy of WRAL News)

Doris Miller, Leeann Magee, Verus Miller,
Pam Baltzell, and Eric Miller, circa 1990
(Courtesy of Verus L. Miller)

in the former neighbor for questioning, but no matter how hard they tried, they could not get her to say anything that connected her to the murder. In the end they had to let her go. To this day Dickerson's case remains a cold case, and one that Morgan could not, and will not, ever let go of. Like every unsolved case, Morgan carries it with him wherever he goes. No matter how many cases he solves, the unsolved ones always stay with him.

"It was one of the great failures—that I still have to wrestle with every night—in my career. We should have broken her. We should have gotten her to confess. We tried our best. I tried my best, and we failed," Morgan says with resignation.

COMING TO THE TABLE

Shortly after the promotion ceremony in the late fall of 2001, another meeting was set up between the Miller family, investigators, and the Wake County District Attorney's Office. Morgan approached this meeting with a sense of "foreboding," considering how poorly the last meeting with the Millers had gone. Since that time little had changed and Morgan could see no good coming out of a sit-down with a grieving family who wanted and needed answers that the investigative team was still in no position to provide.

According to Morgan, Tom Ford and Jeff Fluck were still convinced that the autopsy results were wrong, that there was another toxin involved that had yet to be discovered.

Without the clear scientific evidence to back this theory up, Morgan says Ford was unwilling to pursue the case any further, end of story. Again, Ford made it clear to the Millers that he wasn't willing to pursue the case at that point, as if he hadn't been clear enough in their earlier meeting. Morgan's heart sank.

"I felt like I was in a really bad position. I couldn't really give these people a whole lot of hope. I couldn't really do a whole lot for them in any direction because it just appeared that we had a big mess," he recalls.

For Morgan, it was the moment he realized he had no choice but to work as hard as he could on the Millers' behalf to find some way to take this case to court despite Ford's reluctance. He knew that in the absence of some kind of concrete justice, the Miller family would live the rest of their lives tormented by the knowledge that someone had gotten away with Eric's murder. It was a thought that he couldn't live with.

Eric's family "had the look of people who were experiencing their own sort of death on the inside," Morgan says.

He knew that nothing he did would bring Eric Miller back, and that there was no such thing as "closure" despite the term being grossly overused by the media to describe what victims' families were rewarded with when someone was arrested and subsequently convicted in their loved one's murder.

"These cases are never ever closed for the victim's family," Morgan says angrily. "They're closed for the police department, they're closed for the court system, they're closed for the prosecutors. The lawyers say they're closed, but there's never any closure from the death of your brother, your sister, your wife, your husband, your daughter, your son, you know, your best friend. You never get closure in a case where somebody is murdered. It will always be a gaping, festering wound that will haunt you forever."

Truth was, Morgan couldn't offer them or anyone "closure." He might be able to offer them justice, *that* he just might be able to do, but closure—that would be far too arrogant for Morgan or anyone other than God to take on.

But in order to find justice for the Millers, Morgan knew he would have to do more than simply find a way to get this case into a courtroom; he had to find a new captain to steer the ship. His gut told him that Tom Ford wasn't that person, and would never be that person. But like so many other things that Morgan wanted, this decision wasn't up to him. It was up to the Wake County district attorney, Colon Willoughby.

AN OPENING

Morgan was well aware that shortly before Derril Willard's suicide, he had consulted with the well-known defense attorney and former cop Rick Gammon. Morgan remembered Willard sitting inside the Crown Vic, having a confidential conversation with Gammon on *Morgan's* cell phone. God how Morgan wished he could have been a fly on the wall during that conversation; or for that matter, any conversation between Willard and Gammon.

It struck Morgan that Gammon was probably one of the

only people besides Ann Miller who had concrete information about Eric Miller's murder. He asked Ford whether there was any way to get at that information.

"The more I pondered the question, the more important it had become to me to find out, what did Rick Gammon know?"

Morgan recalls that Ford became almost hysterical at the mere mention of this idea, arguing that there was no way to get at that information, no matter how vital it might be to the case, because it breached the sanctity of attorney-client privilege. Morgan remembers Ford telling him it would violate all of the ethical tenets of Gammon's legal responsibilities to his client. Not being a lawyer, Morgan could only concede that this was another instance where Ford, as much as Morgan hated to admit it, was probably right.

But like everything else Morgan ever felt in his gut, the idea was not going to dissipate easily. He filed it in the back of his mind for the moment, but in his heart he refused to let go of it. In some ways he probably knew then that it could ultimately be the key to unraveling what had become a very complex murder mystery.

TURNING POINT

Like so many other things in Morgan's career as a homicide detective, one case often helped him gain a footing in another.

It was a Friday night, October 26, 2001. Christopher

Holden was teaching his young wife, Sharon Holden, how to load and unload a handgun he had purchased for self-defense. Somehow, the gun went off, shooting Christopher in the chest and killing him. It was up to Morgan's team to decide whether or not the shooting had been an accident or a homicide.

Investigators interviewed Sharon Holden at length. Morgan remembers her as being consistent with her story and appropriately remorseful. Over and over again they asked her whether she meant to kill her husband, or if it was an accident. Every time the answer was the same—that it was an accident. While Morgan was a skeptical man by nature, he also considered himself pretty perceptive about people and their motives. He believed the woman and her story.

"One paradigm that I've always lived by is that the truth makes sense. As far as life, and particularly as it relates to police work," Morgan says bluntly, "if it doesn't make sense, it's not the truth."

In this case it made sense that Sharon Holden had accidentally shot and killed her husband. Interviews with people she knew showed that she appeared to be very much in love with her husband and that there was no evidence of infidelity on either spouse's part.

Morgan called Wake County deputy district attorney Howard Cummings to discuss the case. Cummings was someone Morgan had grown to trust and respect in the D.A.'s office. In short, Morgan felt that Cummings was a person he believed would ultimately do the right thing, not necessarily the politically correct thing, or the popular thing. These traits made the prosecutor a kindred spirit, someone Morgan admired, someone he could speak with honestly about the facts of a case without fear of being criticized.

And unlike so many other attorneys Morgan had dealt with over the years, Cummings had one important quality that stood out—he listened to what you had to say without interrupting.

After hearing Morgan's theory about Christopher Holden's shooting, Cummings agreed that there were no grounds to prosecute Sharon Holden. With the D.A.'s approval, the shooting would be ruled an accident by the Raleigh Police Department. This should have been the end of the case. There was nothing more to say or do. The woman was free and clear. But there was still one more unexpected installment, which had very little to do with this case but very much to do with the Miller case. It would blow the Miller case wide open.

THE PHONE CALL

It's amazing how in police work, as in life, one moment can change everything. A man finds a love note and discovers his wife is having an affair. A routine gossip session at work gets you fired. One too many drinks before getting behind the wheel of your car lands you in jail.

In the Miller homicide there was something missing that could turn the dead-end case into a slam dunk. For

Morgan it was as simple as a phone call. It was a routine night, a routine phone call that put something totally out of the ordinary into Morgan's head, something that had never been done. Afterward, instead of sailing into the wind, all of a sudden he was smoothly gliding along with the current again and could see the horizon for the first time in months.

It was close to Thanksgiving in 2001. Morgan was working the night shift. He got a message to page defense attorney Rick Gammon. Morgan scratched his head and tried to recall whether the police department had any open cases that Gammon was involved in at the moment. He couldn't come up with any. Defense attorneys didn't usually call the police, even when they had a preexisting relationship as Gammon and Morgan did, from their days as beat cops. If they did call, it was usually during business hours, not at night. Morgan was intrigued. He paged Gammon, and Gammon called him back almost immediately.

Gammon told Morgan that he represented the owner of the restaurant where Sharon Holden worked. Gammon went on to describe Sharon as a dedicated employee, and said that his client was concerned about her well-being.

Morgan assured Gammon that the police were ruling the shooting accidental. He told him that Deputy D.A. Howard Cummings was on board with the decision, and that there was nothing more to be done with the case. Morgan recalled that even after this was said, Gammon hung on the line and asked a few more questions. Morgan saw an opening; not a big opening, but an opening.

"I said, 'Rick, while I've got you on the phone, let me

ask you something, buddy: when are you going to tell us what Derril Willard told you?' " Morgan says, knowing full well that even their old police ties wouldn't be enough to make Gammon elaborate. "And to this day I think that was probably one of the true bellwether moments of the Eric Miller investigation because Rick Gammon told me at that point and time, he said, 'I'm never going to be able to tell anybody what I know unless a judge orders me to.' And I stood there for a moment with my mouth open."

Morgan realized that whether he'd done it intentionally or not, Gammon had given him the answer. He'd let him know in a read-between-the-lines manner that in fact there *was* a way to get the information, that it was not *impossible,* as Tom Ford had led him to believe.

The wheels started turning. Morgan knew that Gammon was bound by the ethics of his profession and the guiding principles of attorney-client privilege, but he still pressed on. He wanted to learn as much as he could from Gammon before he hung up the phone. Morgan wanted to know how to kick-start the legal process of getting to the information that Gammon had.

"He knew something that I needed to know, we all needed to know, and I kept feeling very strongly that maybe we'd turned the corner," Morgan says with enthusiasm. "Maybe this case wasn't in the shambles that I once thought it was."

So Morgan did what any good investigator would do. He looked for common ground, an area where Gammon might feel comfortable enough to throw him a bone for old times' sake. He harkened back to their days as beat cops walking the streets of downtown Raleigh together. He reminded Gammon of an old furniture store with a dirty plate-glass window. Depending upon where you stood, you had only a partial view of the inside of the store. The dirty window obstructed certain areas inside the building. He told Gammon to imagine that they were looking through that window again, checking to see if anything untoward was going on in the back of the closed store.

" 'Rick, can you tell me, are you seeing more than what I'm seeing?' And he said, 'Oh yeah, I'm seeing a whole lot more than what you're seeing,' " Morgan says emphatically. "And at that point I knew, I knew how the Eric Miller case would fall down. I knew how it would come together and how we would eventually end up solving it. Rick Gammon was the key."

FINDING THE HOOK

Morgan is very clear to point out that Gammon never crossed the line in that phone call, that he is a stand-up guy who takes his professional ethics and responsibilities very seriously. They had known each other for thirty years, but not even their friendship was enough to make Gammon violate his sacred oath to protect his client.

"I think he [Rick] found a way to straddle the line, staying on the side of doing what was right and what was ethical under his professional guidelines, but he was still able to convey to me what needed to be done," Morgan theorizes. After hanging up, Morgan sat and stared at the dusty pale blue wall in his office for a very long time, trying to sort out the whole conversation.

Morgan didn't know then, and doesn't know to this day, if Gammon planned the opportunity for Morgan to ask him about Willard, or if it all just happened by coincidence. But in the end it really didn't matter. Morgan had caught the pass; now he just needed to figure out how to get to the end zone.

Morgan knew by Tom Ford's exaggerated reaction to the simple mention of the idea in the meeting with the Millers that it could not be raised again in the same context. He needed something more, a heavy-duty hook to hang the big picture on. He needed something to convince a judge that Gammon had critical information that would solve the case, and that it was in the best interest of justice for him to permit Gammon to violate attorney-client privilege this one time.

The answer was actually at Morgan's fingertips, locked away in the stacks of files in a large metal filing cabinet that he still hadn't read completely. His gut had been gnawing at him to *read the files, read the files*. But with everything going on—the promotion, the other murders—he just hadn't had time. Morgan didn't even have time for his family, another pressing issue that was gnawing at him.

But this Christmas, the Christmas of 2001, would be different. For a change, Morgan spent it with his family, and mulled over the Miller case, carefully deciding which road to go down next. What he needed was something to give his idea "traction."

Traction came at an unlikely time, during a winter

storm that completely shut down the city of Raleigh in January 2002. Like most southern cities, Raleigh has very little snow-removal equipment, leaving vehicles paralyzed by the weather (as was law enforcement), but the wheels in Morgan's head were spinning furiously as he took the opportunity to read the complete Miller file.

Morgan cloistered himself in his office and read every document, every medical record, every page, and every note that was in the Miller file. It was in this reviewing of the facts that he had heard so many times, in this tedious exercise in redundancy, that he found what he was looking for, the little kernel of truth that could have been buried had he not bothered to look a little closer. *Thank God for snow,* he thought, *thank God.*

"While I did have my gut feelings, there was a whole lot more to this case than my gut telling me Ann Miller was guilty, was a murderer," states Morgan, recalling just how much evidence investigators had already amassed against the woman.

One of the things Morgan homed in on was multiple interviews with people who'd known Derril Willard. They repeatedly told investigators that Willard's attitude, his outlook on life, had changed drastically in the fall of 2000. This coincided with the time when it appeared Willard began his affair with Ann Miller.

According to the files, Ann's and Willard's colleague, Randy Bledsoe (who was also one of the men from the bowling outing where Eric had first gotten sick), told investigators that Willard had appeared almost clinically depressed during the summer of 2000. Like most of his coworkers, Willard was apparently very concerned about the merger taking place at their company. But Bledsoe said Willard took it harder than the rest of them, that he appeared to be almost suicidal, a situation that deeply concerned his colleagues. But in the early fall of 2000, Bledsoe told investigators, Willard's behavior changed dramatically, that he was practically a different person once Ann started paying attention to him.

Bledsoe told police that Ann's flirtation with Willard lifted him out of his funk. His coworkers were so relieved by Willard's turnaround that they overlooked Ann's obvious pursuit of this vulnerable man.

This made it very clear to Morgan, "crystal clear," that Ann had used Willard as an instrument, a tool, someone she could manipulate in order to accomplish her goal—Eric's death. Ann was the aggressor and Willard was her pawn. Willard's colleagues told investigators that the whole thing was very out of character for Willard, who tended to be quiet and reserved.

When Morgan started to match the time line of Ann's relationship with Willard along with the autopsy information showing that Eric had been poisoned throughout the summer of 2000, he realized that Willard could not have taken part in it since he hadn't been in the picture at that time. To Morgan, this meant that all the little "preview" doses of arsenic Dr. Clark said Eric had received over the summer *had* to have come from Ann.

Medical records contained in the file also piqued Morgan's interest. They contained Eric's clinical diagnosis during each hospitalization. Most of it was Greek to Morgan, but after poring over it time and time again, he got the point. In Morgan's mind what it boiled down to was that although Willard may have *tried* to kill Eric Miller that night at the bowling alley, the dose he gave him was insufficient to do so, it was not a deadly dose. The dose of arsenic that killed Eric Miller came later, a dose given to him by *Ann* alone.

"On that night it was like the stars lined up. Eric's parents were out of the house, he was there alone with Ann and baby Clare," Morgan elaborates. "Ann prepared food for Eric that night. It was the only time that had happened since he had been released from the hospital. It was just too much to be a coincidence. Ann Miller gave Eric that last dose of arsenic the night before he went back into the hospital for the final time."

This scenario fell right in line, as far as Morgan was concerned, with Willard's suicide note disclaiming any responsibility in taking Eric's life. He may have tried to kill Eric at one time, but he failed. Derril Willard didn't kill Eric Miller. He was being honest in his last words to his family and friends.

"The big thing was [that] Ann was alive, Derril was dead. And I still maintain that Ann is at least morally liable for Derril's death. When Ann intervened in his life, she essentially signed his death warrant," Morgan states.

There was another part of the file that recounted interviews detectives had done with Willard's wife, Yvette, on three separate occasions. This ended up to be the gem that

Morgan had been looking for, a clue that had not been discarded, but had been lost beneath a pile of other information. Yvette had told investigators that her husband had not only admitted the affair to her, he'd also specifically told her that he'd had no part in Eric's death. She'd told them she knew that her husband had gone to see Rick Gammon for legal advice. Yvette said that Gammon told her husband he could be charged with attempted murder.

"I kept saying, 'This is it! Why hasn't anybody told me about this before?'" Morgan says incredulously. "I suddenly realized I had found my *in*."

Morgan's hunch had been right all along. Willard had poisoned Eric Miller that night at the bowling alley. But since Miller didn't die that night, Gammon had told his client he could be charged with *attempted* murder, not murder, or conspiracy to commit murder. To Morgan this distinction made perfect sense. Willard was a gentle soul who had been led so far down the garden path by his lust for Ann Miller that he *attempted* to kill the man he perceived to be his romantic rival. But then he quit. It was up to Ann to finish the job.

Morgan knew Gammon was a straight shooter, a good lawyer, one of the best, and that he wouldn't have given Willard bad advice. Gammon didn't tell Willard he could be facing a murder charge because Willard must have told him the whole truth, that Ann had given Eric the deadly dose. This meant that Rick Gammon *knew* Ann was guilty. But it was a secret still locked up tightly in the vault of attorney-client privilege.

THE WIDOW

Morgan is a tough guy with a soft heart. The next step in this case was something he dreaded with a passion, but he knew he had to do it. Before this thing went any further, he needed to talk to Yvette Willard face-to-face, not just read about what she had said to other investigators. He needed to see her for himself, see her expressions, judge her truthfulness, hear the words *attempted murder* roll off her tongue. So he called upon all of his manly courage and made the call.

"I thought there was a strong chance that Yvette Willard probably associated me with her husband's suicide, probably *blamed* me for her husband's suicide," Morgan says. "Undaunted, I summoned all the charm and guile that I had and put in a call to Yvette Willard."

She agreed to meet with Morgan the following Friday night after work. Dr. Michael Teague accompanied Morgan on the visit. Teague was there to observe, but he was also there for moral support. Morgan felt a little like he was treading on a dead man's grave, but at the same time he knew it was something that had to be done.

Morgan figured that from Yvette's point of view, her dead husband's reputation hung in the balance, and nothing, including the arrest of Ann Miller, could bring that reputation back. In fact, the investigation would only continue to further tarnish Willard's memory, something Morgan knew the mother of a young child did not want. He felt sorry for her. In his mind she was also one of Ann's victims. From the little that he knew about Yvette Willard, Morgan honestly believed the woman had tried her best to be a good wife, had tried to keep her marriage and her family together, but Ann's magnetic hold on Derril Willard was just too strong for Yvette to fight.

"I told her what I felt to be the truth. I felt like Derril was essentially a victim in this case, too," Morgan says, recalling how he tried to find common ground with the grieving widow.

And then Morgan asked Yvette Willard the question detectives had asked her before. He asked her if Rick Gammon had really told her that her husband could be charged with attempted murder. She told him emphatically "Yes."

Yvette Willard was the traction Morgan had been looking for.

THE MOMENT OF TRUTH

Who to call? Morgan knew he couldn't call Tom Ford. He would get shut down faster than a bar at closing time. The more he thought about it, the clearer it became. There was certainly one person he was convinced would do the right thing: Deputy District Attorney Howard Cummings.

Cummings always spoke quietly, methodically, often without a trace of emotion in his voice or a hint of expression on his face. It was obvious that he chose his words cautiously. Cummings was a balding man with glasses and a dry wit, sometimes so dry that Morgan couldn't tell when he was being serious or making a joke. Yet beneath his lack of affectation, it had always been clear to Morgan that Cummings paid attention to every word you said. When he listened, he really listened and thoughtfully processed what he heard.

"Howard [Cummings] never appeared to be overenthusiastic. He says, 'Well I need to think about this and the possible implications,' and from there Howard apparently took the bull by the horns and went directly to Colon," Morgan says with admiration.

Morgan knew that District Attorney Colon Willoughby was the only one who could authorize taking the case to the next level. Willoughby was the pilot, while Cummings was his very able and steady copilot.

Willoughby's boyish good looks belied his fiftysomething years. He spoke with a measured southern drawl, walked with an easy gait, and frequently flashed a mischievous smile. He was known as a bright and honest prosecutor whose conservative approach often reined in investigators looking for more immediate results.

Morgan was making one of his periodic checks on Ann Miller in Wilmington, tailing her to be exact, when he got the call that changed everything. It was rotten duty, but someone had to do it. Morgan had decided that even though he was now officially in charge of the unit, he still had to get his hands dirty. He was knee-high in muck when Willoughby called.

"I'll always remember the exact words of our esteemed district attorney. He said, 'Now, is this information that we've just uncovered or is this just something we just realized is there?' " Morgan imitates the D.A.'s words with an exaggerated southern drawl.

Willoughby was a smart man who would have made a great poker player. He rarely ever got ruffled. It was almost impossible to know what he was really thinking. But Morgan knew him well enough to realize that he wouldn't be calling if he wasn't very interested in pursuing this new angle.

Morgan told Willoughby that the information from Yvette Willard had been there all along, but that he had just put two and two together recently after reading the complete case file. He told Willoughby that he felt that this information was the key to getting a judge to compel Gammon to talk because it showed that Willard and Gammon had spoken about something *substantial,* something that might just solve the case. On the other end of his cell phone, there was silence as Willoughby listened intently to what Morgan had to say.

COURT OF PUBLIC OPINION

The more Morgan interacted with Eric Miller's family, the more desperate he became to help them. In his heart he felt that Gammon was the key to pushing the case forward, and now, with Yvette Willard's corroboration of what Gammon had said to her husband, Morgan felt as though it *had* to move forward. Either the D.A. would take it to the next level or Morgan would do so himself.

"I had to give this family something to hope for. I felt like I was essentially backed into a corner. I didn't have a whole lot of ammunition, I didn't have a whole lot to work with," recalls Morgan. "I decided that our next-best strategy was to try the case in the court of public opinion."

Using his contacts in the media, Morgan knew he could get an audience for this story. Just a few simple calls would get all of the local networks scrambling their cameras out the door at his beck and call if he chose to take that route. If the state wouldn't go after Ann Miller, he felt sure that ordinary citizens hearing about the case would go after the state.

Confidentially, Morgan told the Miller family that he intended to have a press conference and reveal the details of the case if the D.A. didn't do something by March 1, 2002. As part of what he called "Plan B," Morgan lined up newspaper and television reporters to be on standby in case Willoughby wouldn't, or for some reason couldn't, pursue this new angle. Unlike other cops who had an innate fear of the media, Morgan knew how to use reporters like they used him. It was a mutually beneficial relationship. He wasn't above exploiting it when it needed to be exploited.

"If Colon [Willoughby] had not taken the bull by the horns, he would have ended up sometime in early March with a hell of a public relations problem," Morgan says. "If Colon wasn't going to do the right thing, then I was going to essentially put him in a position where he was forced to do something."

Luckily, it didn't come to that. Willoughby informed

Morgan that he would file a petition asking the court to compel Gammon to talk. Together, Morgan and Willoughby prepared an affidavit to attach to the petition. They included all of the major details in the case, just as they had done in the affidavit to search Willard's house. But at this point in the investigation, more than a year after the crime, they had amassed many new details that made the case both stronger and more salacious.

Some juicy details, however, were deleted from the affidavit after Willoughby objected. For example, Morgan claims that on the weekend prior to the bowling outing, Derril Willard and Ann Miller had spent a weekend holed up at a Ritz-Carlton in Chicago. Yvette Willard had confirmed this clandestine rendezvous, which Morgan saw as Ann laying the groundwork for getting Willard to poison Eric. Morgan imagined that Ann and Willard had spent the weekend in bed as she tried to convince him to poison her husband. Ann had worked him for months, but it was in that bed, in that hotel room in Chicago, that she broke him. There was no going back.

Morgan says that Willoughby felt that releasing the information about the Chicago weekend would be showing too many cards at one time. Always the stone-faced poker player, he told Morgan that they had to hold something back and Morgan agreed. Morgan was so pleased to finally have Willoughby's support that he would have agreed to just about anything at this point.

"Colon is a hero in this case," praises Morgan with a shit-eating grin.

WHEELS OF JUSTICE

The Miller family had returned to Raleigh for the hearing on Willoughby's petition. While their previous trips to Raleigh had been bittersweet, this one was tinged with a hopefulness that Morgan hadn't seen in them for months.

The courtroom was packed with media from all over the state, along with cops, lawyers, and gawkers. Morgan greeted Rick Gammon with what he called a "manly half hug." Gammon was a small man, with a buzz cut, a neatly trimmed mustache, and an affable personality. He exuded confidence, the kind that let you know he was comfortable with just about anything you could throw at him. He always greeted people with a sincere smile and an easy handshake. *Let the games begin,* Morgan thought.

The judge presiding over the hearing was Judge Donald Stephens, the chief resident Superior Court judge for Wake County. He was a law-and-order judge who steered clear of politics and had gained the respect of the entire legal community. Because he was dedicated to strictly following the law as it was written, and not as many people wanted to interpret it, no one had ever been able to predict how Stephens would rule on any case until the words came out of his mouth. He would often stop witnesses and lawyers in midsentence to ask them pointed questions or to steer them away from a tangent that was going nowhere.

The white-haired, handsome jurist peered down at the courtroom from the bench with his wire-framed glasses perched as always on the tip of his nose. When he became annoyed, Judge Stephens would take the glasses off with one hand and knead his forehead with the other hand.

"There is no better judge that I've had the privilege to appear in front of, or that I know of," Morgan says, echoing the sentiments of almost everybody who knew Donald Stephens. "I've always found him fair. I've always found him truthful and I've always found him to be a proponent of the law and of justice."

One of Gammon's attorneys, a bright, young, aggressive lawyer named Joe Zeszotarski, argued that compelling Gammon to tell the court what Willard had told him would forever tarnish the meaning of attorney-client privilege in North Carolina. Zeszotarski claimed that it would thereafter make it impossible for defense attorneys to gain the trust of their clients and adequately represent them. Morgan knew this argument would be raised, and that it was in fact a good argument. He held his breath and waited to see what Judge Stephens would do with it.

Stephens paused, as he often did, appearing to be in deep thought about what he had just heard. He looked up at the ceiling as if the answer could be hanging there from a low beam where he might just pluck it off. You could almost see his mind working on a counterargument to challenge the young attorney. He asked Zeszotarski whether, if someone had been convicted and sentenced to death and Gammon had information that could prove that person was really innocent, it would be prudent to hand the information over.

"Judge Stephens gave him that sort of halfway grin,

halfway smile, and said: 'Well, is that right?' " Morgan recalls.

It was over, for now at least. Stephens ordered Gammon to tell him everything he knew in the privacy of his own chambers, or *in camera,* to use the legal term. Morgan had no doubt that Gammon had something important to share, and that somehow, Judge Donald Stephens would find a legal way to get that information to investigators.

SEVEN

The impossible is often the untried.
—JIM GOODWIN

"We left that hearing in the Wake County Courthouse that day, myself and the Miller family, with a sense that things were finally on track," Morgan says. "I don't think any of us realized at that point and time just how slow the wheels of justice sometimes turn."

It was clear that Rick Gammon was going to appeal the judge's order mandating him to reveal what he knew about the Miller case. And on March 14, 2002, following proper legal protocol, he did just that. Word on the street was that the case would skip the Court of Appeals and go straight to the North Carolina Supreme Court, but no one knew for sure because this was such a unique case. It was a test of the attorney-client privilege that had the capacity to affect many other cases in the future. Given its gravity, most people close to the case felt it was a legal question which deserved to be heard by the highest court in the state.

In the meantime Morgan was nervous. He had made so many promises to the Millers, to the community, and to himself. If this didn't work, he wasn't sure there was any-place else for him to turn. He would officially be at a dead end in this investigation, and the thought kept him awake at night.

"It was like I had written a very large check and wasn't sure I was ever going to be able to get the funds in the bank to cover it by the time it had made it to the bank," Morgan recalls.

But Morgan just kept hoping that the funds would be there. He prayed that a trip to the North Carolina Supreme Court would mean a big payoff for the Eric Miller case—a payoff in the form of the arrest of Ann Miller on murder charges.

As everyone waited for some kind of resolution to the legal wrangling, the media weighed in on the question of attorney-client privilege. Every night Morgan watched self-proclaimed experts on the evening news arguing that vacating the attorney-client privilege would be the worst thing that could happen in this case—that it would set a le-gal precedent that would have a permanently chilling effect on the attorney-client relationship. But while the pundits sided with the defense, Morgan observed the general pub-lic siding with the state's position, that solving a murder trumped the attorney-client privilege of a dead man. Yvette Willard herself had weighed in on the debate, saying that she *wanted* Gammon to speak, that as the executor of Der-ril Willard's estate, she gave him permission to do so. But under the law, her permission was still not enough for

Gammon to vacate his oath not to share his confidential conversations with his client.

The Millers became media junkies as well, scouring the Internet every day for the latest news on the case. They also, like Morgan, became increasingly disturbed by the fact that so many lawyers were deciding the outcome of the case before the courts had a chance to even consider the question.

Morgan couldn't understand it no matter which way he looked at it. He felt strongly that what the state was asking for was a narrowly defined exception to the attorney-client privilege in a case where the client was deceased. It wasn't as if Derril Willard was going to sue. Morgan had always felt that the end result, getting a killer off the street, was worth whatever small breach of attorney-client privilege would result from this case.

"By that time in my career, like it or not, whether it was a good thing or not, I guess I had become something of a public figure," Morgan says with bravado. "People recognized me. I'd be standing in line at the convenience store and people that I'd never seen before, didn't know, would come up and say, 'I think you all are doing the right thing and I just don't understand why they can't make that lawyer talk.'"

One late night Morgan stopped by a grocery store on his way home from work to pick up a few items. While he was standing in line a woman he didn't recognize tapped him on the shoulder and identified herself as the wife of a prominent local attorney. She told him she thought he should keep pushing, that he was going in the right direction, that he was "doing the right thing." She hugged him as she exited the store and left Morgan thinking he must be doing something right if the folks from the other side of the battlefield were wishing him well.

THE LETTER

The Millers were frustrated that there was little they could do to influence the courts. But they felt strongly that they had the ability to influence public opinion. So Verus and Doris Miller wrote a letter to the community at large and distributed it through the media. Morgan wholeheartedly supported their decision to make this painful and emotional public statement. He had been around long enough to know that while judges were supposed to ignore public sentiment when making their decisions, they, too, were human beings with feelings, human beings who read the newspaper and watched television news.

THE LOSS OF ERIC MILLER
LIFE WITHOUT ANSWERS. LIFE WITHOUT HOPE. AND
WORST OF ALL— LIFE WITHOUT OUR SON ERIC.
    PLEASE STOP FOR JUST ONE MOMENT. THOSE
OF YOU WITH SONS AND DAUGHTERS, STOP AND
THINK OF LIFE WITHOUT YOUR CHILD. IT IS UN-
BEARABLE, AND I AM SURE THAT YOU DO NOT
WANT TO EXPERIENCE THAT FEELING AGAIN.
    OUR FAMILY HAS BEEN PATIENT, BUT WE ARE
BEGINNING TO TIRE. IT HAS BEEN A VERY LONG

AND PAINFUL 16 MONTHS. IS TRUTH AND JUSTICE FOR ERIC TOO MUCH TO ASK? WE HAVE PAID THE ULTIMATE PRICE AND JOINED A CLUB IN WHICH NO ONE WANTS TO BE A MEMBER. WE ARE WEA-RIED OF THE LACK OF ANSWERS AND WANT SOME PEACE AND RESOLUTION. SOME OF THE FACTS IN THIS CASE ARE ALL TOO CLEAR, BUT THE PRIMARY QUESTION, THE ONE THAT CAUSES US FITFUL, RESTLESS NIGHTS IS WHY? WHY DID ERIC HAVE TO DIE? IS THE COOPERATION OF EVERYONE WHO MIGHT BE ABLE TO HELP ANSWER THIS QUESTION TOO MUCH TO ASK?

THINK OF ALL THE SONS AND DAUGHTERS WHO HAVE GIVEN THEIR LIVES SO THAT WE CAN HAVE FREEDOM IN A COUNTRY WHERE TRUTH AND JUS-TICE SHOULD PREVAIL. HAVE THESE LIVES BEEN LOST FOR NOTHING?

THE QUESTION REGARDING THE PRIVILEGE OF COMMUNICATION BETWEEN AN ATTORNEY AND HIS CLIENT IS NOW MAKING ITS WAY TO THE AP-PELLATE COURTS OF NORTH CAROLINA. IT IS ONE OF A VERY DIFFICULT NATURE, WE FULLY UNDER-STAND THIS. WHILE WE ARE NOT LAWYERS OR JUDGES, WE PRAY THAT THE JUSTICES OF THE COURT OF APPEALS AND THE SUPREME COURT WILL GIVE THE MATTER DUE CONSIDERATION, IN A TIMELY MANNER. WE KNOW THAT DERRIL WILLARD'S FAMILY WANTS ANSWERS TOO.

WE SHOULD ALL COME TOGETHER WHEN A FAMILY NEEDS HELP, HELP IN FINDING ANSWERS.

*AFTER ALL, WE ARE ALL HUMAN BEINGS WITH
FAMILIES AND LOVED ONES. WE APPRECIATE ALL
OF THE CARING AND SUPPORT THAT OUR FAMILY
HAS RECEIVED FROM THE RALEIGH COMMUNITY,
AND WE PRAY THAT EVERYONE WILL BE DILIGENT
IN HELPING US TO FIND ANSWERS AND TO SEEK
JUSTICE FOR OUR SON ERIC. HE WAS A MAN OF
GREAT WORTH AND GREAT LOVE FOR EVERYONE.
WE ALL NEED TO KNOW WHY HE IS NO LONGER
AMONG US.*

FAMILY TIES

"To be honest with you, I think I was just as fearful as they
were," Morgan admits.

He had tried to keep in touch with the family on a regular basis and kept them as informed as he could about the
case, but it was hard. He had other murders to solve. He was
only one man with a staff of detectives who were already
working overtime on several other cases. But like every
other case he had been involved in, he walked a fine line between being a detective investigating their son's murder,
and a man who had become their close, personal friend.

"I had tried to be as careful as I could to maintain a professional relationship, which I always did," Morgan says
like a man trying to convince himself. "With a case as
complicated, as heart-wrenching, as Eric Miller's, I mean I
couldn't leave these people out there flapping in the
breeze."

He had bonded with Beth-Ellen Vinson's family. He had bonded with Eric Miller's family. He had bonded with Beulah Dickerson's family. Morgan simply didn't know any other way to do his job. It was impossible for him to get the victims or their loved ones out of his mind.

"Sometimes I'd just be drawn back to Wicker Drive . . . where Beth-Ellen Vinson's body had been found, and I would sit there, park my car, walk over the actual exact spot where Beth-Ellen's body had been found, and almost will her ghost, her spirit, to come and give me some kind of guidance," says Morgan uncharacteristically. He was not a man who was naturally prone to put much stock in the supernatural.

He did the same thing with Beulah Dickerson's house, driving way out of his way on his way home from work to "swing by" Pine View Drive one more time, hoping something would come to him, something he had not seen before.

It was around this time, the spring of 2002, that the district attorney's office officially pronounced the Dickerson case dead in the water. Morgan met with several assistant district attorneys who told him there was simply not enough probable cause to charge his suspect, Dickerson's former neighbor.

"Same old story; I'd heard it before and I was getting kind of tired of it," grouses Morgan with a chip on his shoulder the size of California.

But he wasn't tired of the victims' families. Truthfully, he felt privileged that they allowed him into their homes and their lives, and shared their very personal sorrow with him. Yet at the same time he felt helpless. At this point it looked as if there was nothing he could *ever* do for the Dickersons, and there was nothing at the moment he could do for the Millers. The legal process was slow as molasses, and while it dripped one lonely drop at a time, the investigations had both come to standstills.

Morgan acknowledges that for victims' families, the loss becomes the biggest and most significant part of their lives. Given this fact, allowing them to be involved in the investigation, even in the tiniest way, went a long way toward helping them heal because it made them feel useful.

In order to maintain their precious relationship with Clare—their only connection to Eric—the Miller family continued to have a relationship with Ann. It was close to impossible for them to interact with the woman they felt sure had murdered their son and brother, but they did it for Eric's daughter. Morgan admired their cool detachment in dealing with Ann for the greater good of the relationship with their granddaughter and niece.

The entire Miller family, including Eric's sisters, had kept up a brave front all along for the sake of Clare. Because neither grandparents nor aunts have any legal custody rights to a child unless specifically granted by a judge, Ann was their gatekeeper to Clare. They *had* to have a relationship with her in order to have access to the child. But at the same time their rage grew as they learned about the growing body of evidence against Ann.

But then the Millers went one step beyond just keeping

the peace. With Morgan's help they became pseudo investigators, hoping to glean something from Ann Miller that the police had missed, something that only someone who knew her could get out of her. They were fed up with waiting and decided to join the search for answers.

CALLING THE DEVIL

On March 13, 2002, Pam Baltzell, Eric's sister, called Ann Miller at her home in Wilmington. This was no typical phone call.

Without Ann's knowledge, Pam taped the telephone call as she probed Ann about the case. Because North Carolina is a one-party state, meaning that only one person needs to be aware of the taping, Pam was completely within her legal rights to undertake this bit of sleuthing. She later shared the tape with the Raleigh Police Department. Below are excerpts from that call.

PAM: What do you have to say about it?

ANN: What do you mean what do I have to say about it?

PAM: Well, you know, Rich [*Pam's husband*] and I were just down here and we asked you about Willard. You told us he was stalking you, and we're just trying to understand what this is about in this affidavit. [*Pam is referring to the police affidavit that had indicated a relationship between Ann and Derril Willard.*]

ANN: I guess I haven't read an affidavit, you know I haven't read anything about— [*Pam cuts her off.*]

PAM: You haven't seen what's out in the papers?

ANN: Pam, I don't read the papers. I had the media chasing me down at work today. I just don't read the papers. I stay away from all of it. You can't, I don't believe what I read in the papers and I don't you know, I just stay away from the papers.

PAM: I mean, what do you think Gammon has to say? I mean, they're pretty hot and heavy on getting him to talk, I mean— [*Ann turns the tables and cuts Pam off.*]

ANN: I have no idea. [*Ann is clearly done with the conversation at this point.*] Yeah, they chased me down at work about it today, so, you know, I just—

PAM: They did? Did you talk to them?

ANN: No!

PAM: Who chased you down?

ANN: Media.

PAM: The media?

ANN: Chased me through parking decks, shoved cameras and microphones in my face. You know, I don't think, I think everybody thinks that I'm just, I mean it's very extremely upsetting and stressful, and you know, I just . . . [*Ann's voice wells up with tears and trails off.*]

Morgan had tipped off a local television news crew from WRAL-TV in Raleigh about where Ann was working and what kind of car she drove. Reporter Len Besthoff had aggressively pursued Ann in the parking garage as she tried to get to her car, shouting questions at her that she refused to answer. To the general public it might have appeared that Ann was being attacked, harassed, unjustly accused, her privacy invaded, but Morgan knew better.

"I thought it was time to take the gloves off and once again, sometimes when your hands are tied in every other direction, you have to use the resources that are available," Morgan says, referring to his friends in the media.

PAM: You know, I mean I can understand that. [*Pam is obviously trying to appear sympathetic in order to gain some common ground.*]

ANN: You, I don't think, I don't think you can. You can't understand it, and you know, even when I know it's coming, and I'm told, look, the media are probably going to come get you and to talk to you. Until you are chased down, chased to your car, chased back into your office with cameras and bright lights and microphones and people shouting at you, shoving them in your face, you can't understand it. As much as I think, okay, this could happen someday and I'm going to be prepared, I can't stop shaking. It took me four hours to stop shaking and to stop crying. And I don't think anybody can understand that. It happens to you, you can't understand it, and even in my head I think, well, I can be prepared for this, but you can't until it, you know, and it's not, and everybody goes, they get the media all stirred up and they get everything all stirred up, and you can't understand what it's like, you know.

PAM: Well, I might not know about the media but I do know how stressful all this is because, you know, we just want the whole thing over.

ANN: That's all I want, too. [*She sounds sincere.*] You have no idea how badly I want this over. You know, and I have to, I have to plan to camp out for the next three or four days at Danielle's house. I mean it's just insane, just insane. I've lived out of a suitcase more in the past year and a half, or year than I have— You know, I just, nobody has any idea. They just, I don't know what everybody thinks, but nobody, I don't think it ever has occurred to anybody how hard this is. [*Ann's voice cracks like a boy going through puberty.*]

PAM: Well what I don't understand is if you don't want to live like that—

ANN: If I don't want to live like this, I should just go to the police and talk to them and I won't have to live like this? Do you think I have anything to tell the police I didn't tell them a year ago? You think anything has changed in my life in the past year?

PAM: I don't know.

ANN: I talked to the police a year ago. I have a lawyer who has asked me not to; you know they took things. They have taken things that my parents have said and twisted them. They have taken things that my friends have said and twisted them. [*Ann sounds defensive.*]

PAM: Like what? [*Pam sounds genuinely interested.*]

ANN: An officer dressed in blue is not a friend— [*Ann laughs nervously*] —to me and you, I'm sorry. I don't mean to be cynical, but they've done nothing but take things people had said and twisted them.

PAM: Like what? I don't understand.

ANN: You know, you know, stuff my dad has talked to Rich about, stuff, they've told one person one thing and another person another thing, and you know, there's things they have—truth they have twisted. You know, even my grandmother. They interviewed my grandmother and my grandmother caught them in a lie. I can't sit here and list them, but . . . [*Ann sounds flustered.*]

PAM: Okay. [*Pam quietly nudges Ann to go on.*]

ANN: The more . . . the more I say, the more there is for them to twist. [*Ann speaks in a little-girl voice.*] They just take every word and do whatever they want with it. Same with my phone, I don't even like talking on my phone. I don't use phones unless I have to. [*She chuckles.*] Because we all know my lines are so incredibly tapped that it's insane. You know, and this is how I live, each phone conversation, every move I make, every conversation I make is all trashed, everything, it's hell, a living hell. And I don't think anybody has a clue.

PAM: I just don't think people understand— [*Pam interrupts Ann's stream of consciousness.*]

ANN: Can you imagine living and knowing that every conversation you have is being tape-recorded and kept in some big machine? You know, can you

imagine going through life like that? And I'm thinking, you know, if anybody wants this over, Pam, you
have got to realize I want this over.

Morgan thoroughly enjoyed the idea that Ann Miller
thought her phones were being bugged. In reality, he wasn't
that good. Getting a wiretap order from a state court in
North Carolina was about as easy as getting a cab in New
York City during rush hour. It was close to impossible, but
clearly Ann believed her phones were tapped, and that gave
Morgan a great deal of satisfaction.

"I can remember on several occasions when we were
following her, we would see her making cell-phone calls
while she was driving through traffic and then all of a sudden, for no apparent reason, Ann would pull over and pull
up to a pay phone at a convenience store and use the pay
phone." Morgan chuckles about her paranoia. "That's just
so out there."

PAM: Well, how are we—how are you going to get it
over? I mean, what do your attorneys say about it? I
mean, they want you just to keep living like this?

ANN: They just tell me to take a day at a time. And to not
worry about tomorrow, but just take a day at a time
and that's all I ever try to do. Actually, they tell me
to take more like a minute at a time, an hour at a
time. And now the media even knows where I
worked. I don't even know how they figured that
one out. The only people—the only people that
know where I worked was you and the police. So

I'm thinking, okay, who called the media [about] where I work? You know, and I just—did you tell them where I worked?

PAM: Did I tell them where you worked? [She *repeats the question incredulously.*]

ANN: Did anybody tell the media where I worked?

PAM: I didn't tell them.

ANN: How did they chase them down at my employment?

PAM: I don't know. I mean, Rich found out where you worked when he was down there before. So it's probably not hard if they really want to do it.

Like a seasoned investigator, Pam Baltzell probed her sister-in-law, asking her the same questions over and over again, each time in different ways. Most of all she let the silences breathe, hoping that Ann would feel compelled to fill them. These were the desperate measures of a grieving sister, a grieving family, willing to go straight to the devil to get the answers they needed.

ANN: You know, I can't answer questions or anything. I've tried to be very— [*Ann ends her sentence midstream with nervous laughter.*]

PAM: And I don't understand that. Why can't you answer these questions? [*Pam sounds exasperated.*] It's out in the newspapers that you called Willard like—I don't know how many times. And that you called him, you were on the phone with him two hours before Eric died at one in the morning! What is that all about? I'm sorry to be so upset about this, but I

mean, I just don't understand. I mean we were just
down there two weeks ago and you said this guy
was stalking you.

Ann struggled to describe her relationship with Willard
to Pam without giving away too much. She revealed little
in the way of facts about the case, but in Morgan's opinion
she revealed a *lot* about her character. When Pam turned
the tape over to Morgan, it gave him a great deal of insight
into just who Ann Miller was, *and* who she was pretending
to be: a victim who refused to take responsibility for anything that had happened. She was a woman who appeared
to be either a fantastic liar or totally in denial that she had
done anything wrong. One thing was clear to Morgan: Ann
Miller thought she was being unjustly persecuted by the
police and the media.

ANN: *Obsessed* might have been a good word [*she is referring to Willard's feelings for her*], but there's a
difference between the two and so—but I don't
know, you know. I don't know what you want me to
say.

PAM: I wanted you to tell us what happened. [*There is
growing rage in her voice.*] What this is all about?

ANN: Would it make any difference? [*Ann sounds smug.*]
Would anybody listen to me?

PAM: Yes, we're listening, that's why—

ANN: I don't think so. [*Ann cuts Pam off.*] I really don't. I
really don't. I really don't think anybody would listen to me.

PAM: Yes, we would!

ANN: No, I really don't think you would, Pam.

PAM: Why, why?

ANN: I just don't feel like you guys—I don't think you have given me a chance or, you know. [*Ann punctuates each pause with nervous laughter.*] I think, and your parents, you read the papers and you've already—you already have foregone conclusions in your head about—I don't think, I think I could talk until I was blue in the face and I don't think—

PAM: Ann, you're not telling us anything. And what you just told Rich and I about the stalking doesn't make sense now with what was just put in the papers this week. And we're just trying to understand. [*Pam's tone softens.*]

ANN: I said that the man was obsessed and I will leave it at that.

PAM: Why were you calling him back, then?

ANN: We were friends.

PAM: At one in the morning before Eric died? [*Pam sounds flabbergasted.*]

ANN: You remember they told us not too long before that they figured out what it was and that they were going to, you know, and I was . . . I don't . . . I'm not going there. [*She gives a hearty, knowing chuckle.*]

PAM: Why not, how are we going to get through this? How are we ever going to get through this?

ANN: I don't know [*she says flatly.*]

PAM: Don't you want this over?

ANN: I pray about that every day. I do want it over. I want this over more than anybody. You have no idea how much I want this over. You're not the one who has media chasing you down; you're not the one that drives around dark alleys trying to get into your home. You're not the one who has police coming. You're damn straight I want this over. I want this over more than anybody. For myself and for Clare and for both of us. 'Cause I can't keep on living like this. I want it over. [*Ann sounds tearful.*]

PAM: You know if you would just talk to the police, and talk to people, they wouldn't be thinking all of this stuff.

ANN: I have told Wade [*Wade Smith, her attorney*] a long time ago that I will do anything that he tells me to and I told the police and I did, I sat down and I talked to them for a while. And I told Wade, I said, you know, I've hired you, whatever you say from here on out. I have wanted to talk to them and he has just asked me for now to not. I don't—he's just asked for me to not.

PAM: Okay. [*Pam sounds resigned.*] Well, I just—I just had to call and talk you about this. It was just, um, you know, quite a bit different than our conversation before.

Pam tried to bring the conversation back to Clare, someone they could talk about without animosity. Pam asked Ann how Clare was sleeping and how she was feeling. But the detour lasted just a few moments before the conversation returned to the virtual elephant in the middle of the room.

ANN: I wish there was something that I could say or give you or do, or something you know, but it—you just have to understand that I do want this to be over.

PAM: It's just hard, this stuff is just all sprouting in the news, people ask us about it. You know, what can we say? We don't have anything to say. Except—

ANN: I mean it's hard, and it's hard and I'm just thinking of Clare, keep thinking about how all of this is, you know. I wish . . . I have this attorney and I have to let him do his job. That's all I can say. You know. He has been doing what he's been doing for forty-some-odd years and he's seen more police, and you know, I don't know, but he's seen more police damage more innocent lives than he has not. You know? And I really feel that he has mine and Clare's interest at heart here. So I have to trust him. I just have to trust him and I'm just doing what he's telling me to do because I do trust him and I have faith in him and I watch the police and I watch them tearing at our families and it's hurtful, you know. And you asked when you were here, you said: "What are you going to tell Clare?"

PAM: Yeah.

ANN: And I'm, like, what do you think Clare—what, Clare's going to go on the Internet, she's going to pull up newspapers and she's going to see, and she's going to know that this tension has existed between our families and stuff, too, that's going to be—that's going to be harder on her than any of it, I think, don't you think?

PAM: I think—I don't—it's going to be hard on her, that's why I asked the question, you know, um, 'cause what is she—what are we going to tell her?

ANN: You know, if she asks where her grandparents were or why, you know, why there was no communication really between the families, that in and of itself is going to be one the hardest things to talk to her about.

PAM: No, we're—we're working on it now, but it's difficult to get through. [*Pam speaks with obvious restraint.*]

ANN: You know.

PAM: Yeah.

ANN: It's just—it's just painful and it's painful that—she is just such a jewel and I just—I just wish you guys had more faith in me and what I feel.

PAM: Well, Ann, we'd like to but it's just hard with the stuff that we read and then when we do ask you about it—

ANN: So many other people have faith in me. So many other people have faith in me. And there are people that have faith in me that I would have expected that you would have had faith in me before—no, even, so, you know, it's just, I struggle with that and it's just really hard for me, so . . .

PAM: Ann, I did have faith in you and I sat in that police department and I defended you when they started asking me questions and that was back in December after Eric died. And then we kept seeing, you know, you wouldn't go talk to them and you wouldn't co-operate with them and then this stuff comes out— [*Pam's tone turns angry.*]

ANN: Don't think it was because I didn't want to, it's be-cause I was told not to. You have to understand that, it's not because I didn't want to, it's always been because I was told not to.

PAM: So after a while we kept getting this other data and we don't get the information from you and it's hard to keep that faith. So I just want you to understand our side of it, too.

ANN: Yeah, but there's other people, too, that don't have a hard time with it.

PAM: Who, your immediate family? [*Pam's growing an-noyance is evident.*]

ANN: No, I have friends and I have a lot of people that— [*Ann's voice drops off midsentence.*]

PAM: But you've got to understand, too, Eric was my brother.

ANN: I understand that, he was my husband. And I loved him very, very, very, very, very much.

PAM: Then why don't you go and try to help find out what happened?

ANN: Because I have a lawyer who has told me not to. I'm trying; I want to know what happened. I have a lawyer—

PAM: Well, I just don't understand his technique then,

Ann. Because it sounds like your life is pretty
crappy right now.

ANN: It is really crappy.

PAM: And if he's doing such a good job, why is your life
so crappy? So, well, hey, thanks for calling me
back. I know you've got to take care of Clare.
[*Pam wraps up the conversation with resignation.
It doesn't appear that Ann is going to break, not
now, not ever.*]

Morgan insists he never instructed the family to make the
calls or to tape them. Verus Miller did the same, calling
Ann's sister Danielle and mining her for anything that might
help the case. In the end the tapes were just more pieces of
the puzzle that Morgan hoped to use to help convince the
D.A., and ultimately a jury, that Ann was guilty of murdering her husband. In his opinion they showed a woman in total denial who dodged the truth at every turn.

"I think it gave us all a preview what her likely defense
would be," Morgan says cryptically.

DEATH OF AN ANGEL

Every victim was important to Chris Morgan. He did not
categorize their worth based on gender, age, race, or edu-
cation. To him each one of them was unique, with their
own set of individual qualities that made them memorable.
He had no hierarchy when it came to murder victims, but

some victims, like Eric Miller and Beth-Ellen Vinson, had managed to gain a foothold on Morgan's heart, a grip so intense even he couldn't explain it.

In the spring of 2002, Morgan added Stephanie Bennett to that list of victims he couldn't forget. The small-town girl from Virginia, a recent college graduate, had just started her life in Raleigh. It was a life full of promise and potential. On May 21, 2002, Stephanie was found raped, tortured, and murdered in her apartment. The killer left his DNA all over the crime scene as if to thumb his nose at investigators and say "catch me if you can." Despite looking at hundreds of DNA samples that were already on file with the state, looking for a match, Raleigh police came up with nothing.

"It was the tragic murder of a young innocent victim [who] through no fault of her own had ended up dying a horrible tragic death," Morgan remembers, his voice heavy with remorse.

Soon after Bennett's murder, on June 28, 2002, Morgan got word that the Miller case had bypassed the North Carolina Court of Appeals and would go straight to the North Carolina Supreme Court for consideration. This was great news, since it meant that things were finally moving ahead. But it was bittersweet. Morgan was one step closer to finding justice for Eric Miller, and yet he felt like he kept taking three steps back in the Stephanie Bennett case.

The main difference between the Bennett case and the Miller case was the amount of concrete physical evidence. Morgan knew that if he could only make a DNA match, he could solve the Bennett case. There would be no argument with the district attorney about the strength of the case or the evidence. This case was a winner, a slam dunk. But unlike the Miller case, he didn't have a suspect.

"Concrete, hard evidence that is irrefutable doesn't come along like that every day," Morgan laments.

But concentrating on the Bennett case had a downside. The case was hot, and Morgan felt like he had to stay on top of it. He had given Eric Miller everything he could for the moment, and the future of the case now rested in the hands of the North Carolina Supreme Court. So he went all out on the Bennett case. This, in turn, concerned the Millers and made them feel like he was putting Stephanie before Eric, while in Morgan's mind they were both angels in heaven on an equal footing who both deserved his focus, but not always constant attention.

Morgan recalls one typical bright and sunny Carolina summer day when he got a call from Verus Miller on his cell phone. Naturally Verus wanted to know why he had not heard from the investigator recently. Morgan was at a loss to explain to his now dear friend why Eric's murder had taken a temporary backseat.

"You always have a situation where they feel like you're *their* detective, that this is your job and that, 'What are you doing working on somebody else's case? You're *my* detective. You don't need to be working on somebody else's case; you need to be working on my case,'" Morgan explains with sympathy.

Morgan was committed to getting justice for Eric Miller *and* Stephanie Bennett. There were not enough hours in the day to make it all happen quick enough, but he would make it happen, somehow, some way.

48 HOURS

Morgan was a friend to the local media. He very rarely turned down interviews, and often solicited their help in cases where he needed it. He saw his relationship with reporters as mutually beneficial. He knew when to use them and how to do it without saying too much. Many of his colleagues were afraid of this kind of attention, afraid of saying the wrong thing, afraid of saying too much. It was a delicate balance. To Morgan it was an *art*.

"It can also be, as I've seen in numerous cases, a terrible, terrible detriment to doing your job if you don't try to learn how to work with the media instead of trying to work against it," Morgan admits.

When a producer for *48 Hours,* Chuck Stevens, first contacted him about the Eric Miller case, Morgan was cautious. But at the same time he saw the value in putting the case in the national spotlight, where everyone, including the district attorney and the North Carolina Supreme Court, could not ignore it.

In hindsight Morgan realizes that he should have told his supervisors, especially Chief Perlov, and probably also the D.A. about his plan to go national. But he moved forward with a single-minded goal, to take all of the bits and pieces that had been previously reported in the Miller case and put them together in a nice neat package that the public could digest.

Morgan knew that Ann Miller's attorneys, particularly Joe Cheshire, a veteran defense attorney and media spin doctor, would soon be jumping on the media train themselves, spinning their version of the story.

So in the midst of working ten to twelve hours a day on the Bennett case, Morgan agreed to take part in the *48 Hours* segment about the Eric Miller case.

Be careful what you wish for, Morgan would think to himself years later. He anticipated a small crew, maybe two or three people, not unlike the local media he was used to dealing with on a regular basis. Having experienced only local television coverage, he expected the whole thing would take about an hour of his time. He was not familiar with the overabundance of resources and demands that accompanied the national media.

As he walked into the police station on the day of the shoot, Morgan noticed people unloading a tractor trailer full of equipment at the front door. He thought nothing of it until he got off the elevator on the fourth floor and saw the media circus unfolding before him. They had turned the Major Crimes Squad Room into a full-blown television studio, complete with scorching bright lights, big fancy cameras, lots of wires, and bodies everywhere. As he sauntered through the hallway to his office, Morgan received a lot of sideways glances and jeers from his coworkers, who were not impressed by what they perceived as Morgan's grandstanding. Clearly, they were more than just a little perturbed by the disruption.

Later that same day, after hours of interviews inside the station, the news crew converted Morgan's unmarked police car into a television studio on wheels. They took all of the junk from his backseat so that the reporter could interview Morgan while he drove with a camera lens just inches from his face in the front seat.

"Very good people, very nice people, very interested and invested people, but they were also people with an agenda, a schedule, and an awful lot of equipment," Morgan recalls with a chuckle and a tinge of embarrassment for the haranguing he got from the other cops.

Russ Mitchell, the reporter, had interviewed the Miller family in Indiana before he came to see Morgan. He knew a great deal about the case and impressed Morgan with his thorough research and preparation.

Naturally he asked Morgan *the* question: "Why haven't you made an arrest in this case?" It was a question that the local media had already asked him hundreds of times. It was a question he'd asked himself every day since Eric Miller's murder. It was a question that, in his heart, he truly had no answer for, but when a television camera was pointed in his direction, he was forced to come up with *something*. So he rambled on about "making progress in the case" and about "working closely with the district attorney's office." Anyone who read between the lines would know that he was implying that his hands were tied and that he was waiting for an okay from the D.A. in order to move forward.

When Morgan told District Attorney Colon Willoughby about the news segment, Willoughby was less than enthusiastic about the prospect of the story making national headlines. Willoughby was a conservative D.A. who took his oath not to speak about an ongoing case in specific terms very seriously. He didn't like loose cannons, especially loose cannons who could possibly jeopardize a case with loose talk. But Morgan assured Willoughby that he had not crossed any lines.

"I kind of looked at the *48 Hours* deal as an insurance policy, a little added motivation in my quest for justice for Eric Miller," Morgan says with a snicker. "It's hard to duck a story or hope it will go away once it's been on a national news program."

Morgan wasn't as prepared for the interview as he should have been, nor was he prepared for the fallout later when the segment aired. Again, he had been used to the local media but not the national spotlight. He had figured a camera was a camera—what was the big deal?

"Looking back on it, I probably should have gotten a better haircut." Morgan laughs. "I think in the end probably my lack of consideration, preparation, and planning—I hope that I came off just as I hoped I would, as somebody who was honestly doing the best that he could in a very difficult quest for justice for Eric Miller."

One thing Morgan tried to stress in the interview was the hundreds of hours of work put in by his detectives. Some people thought Morgan took too much credit for solving cases. He was fully aware of this perception. When you have a bigger-than-life personality, people either love you or hate you, and Morgan had experienced his fair share of hate. But he truly respected and admired the work his squad had done on the case and wanted that to be known in this interview. Morgan's gut told him a lot, but without all of the grunt work done by his detectives, none of his cases would ever have seen their way into a courtroom.

"The work that I did was tenfold done by them [detectives], I mean they did ten times the actual nuts-and-bolts work I did," Morgan states matter-of-factly. "They're a dedicated bunch of men and women who deserve all the credit in the world. I don't think I mention that often enough."

THE HIGH COURT

Finally, on October 15, 2002, it was time for the North Carolina Supreme Court to hear arguments on the Gammon issue. Morgan had never been to the Supreme Court and was duly impressed with the upscale surroundings. He was used to disposable cups, a packed audience in T-shirts and cut-offs, and the constant din of attorneys passing in front of the bench trying to settle cases.

Instead, he walked into a room full of grace and quiet elegance. The stately, historic courtroom with its high ceilings, oil paintings, and freshly polished dark wood was a far cry from a tired Wake County Superior Courtroom. He marveled at the fact that each of the justices had his or her own crystal goblet full of not just water, but *ice water*.

"It's a different world. I tried to go in there with as much dignity as I could wearing my best black fedora," says Morgan humbly.

Colon Willoughby and Bud Crumpler from the North Carolina Attorney General's Office argued for the state. Morgan felt their arguments were strong and impressive. But Gammon's attorneys had equally strong arguments.

" 'Isn't this going to have a chilling effect on the ability of lawyers to represent people effectively?' " Morgan recalls one of the justice's asking. " 'If we give you this, isn't the confidentiality of what someone tells his lawyer always going to be in question?' "

But over and over, Morgan says Crumpler and Willoughby answered these questions simply and directly. They told the justices this was a narrowly defined contingency for this particular case and would not affect state law in a broad and sweeping way.

Every Friday after the North Carolina Supreme Court met regarding the case, Morgan logged on to their Web site to scan the decisions, hoping the judges would hand down something in the Miller case. Back in Indiana, the Miller family was doing the same thing. But every time they checked, there was nothing. It was as if the case had been heard and then *poof*, it simply vanished off the radar screen. The court had no legal mandate to consider the case in a specified amount of time. So Morgan and the Millers waited, and waited, and waited.

"I kept thinking, what in the hell is taking them so long with this?" Morgan says.

GOING NATIONAL

On December 11, 2002, viewers across the country learned details about the Eric Miller case courtesy of Chris Morgan on *48 Hours*. While the story was about Eric Miller, the CBS producer had built the segment around Morgan and his bigger-than-life persona. As it was told through Morgan's eyes, a compelling and passionate backdrop, viewers connected more readily with the case in North Carolina, far away from where most of them lived. Morgan made them care about Eric Miller.

On the night the segment aired, Morgan's family gathered in the den to watch. Morgan himself retreated to his makeshift office in an old shed behind the house to watch alone. He wanted to see for himself whether or not he had screwed up, and he didn't need his family by his side pointing out his blunders.

While it was tough at moments to hear things he wished he hadn't said, or wished he had said differently, he was not disappointed with the results. In the end he had done exactly what he'd set out to do, to put Eric Miller's face on the national map, and to put Ann Miller squarely in the national hot seat.

"If I had thought about it a little bit more, I probably would have never done it. But in retrospect I felt like it was just as an essential part in this process in seeking justice for Eric Miller as anything else we had done in the case," Morgan says. Morgan had always been hot on Ann Miller's trail. She knew it, the D.A. knew it, and now the rest of America knew it.

EIGHT

Beware the fury of a patient man.
—JOHN DRYDEN

The day after his fifteen minutes of fame aired, Morgan was in line at the snack bar in the municipal building getting his usual, a tuna-fish sandwich to go. Everyone was talking about the *48 Hours* segment. Some people ribbed him, others gave him a pat on the back, and others snickered about it behind his back. But at least they were talking about it, and that's what he had hoped for. He wanted people to keep talking about the Eric Miller case because that was the only way to keep it alive.

The whispers didn't bother Morgan; he'd experienced it all before. What did worry him, however, was running into Chief Jane Perlov. When he saw her in line at the snack bar, he assumed that she'd probably seen the segment and would have a strong opinion about it one way or the other. Perlov, not unlike Morgan, seemed to have a strong opinion on just about everything.

In contrast to Morgan, Perlov was a petite woman with short blond hair, the kind of woman people referred to as a "pistol" or a "firecracker." Unlike her predecessors, she always dressed in uniform, a throwback to her days as a beat cop. Morgan supposed that by dressing in uniform, she was trying to send the message that she was one of them, yet there was something about her that could strike fear in the heart of even a large man like himself.

If she didn't say anything, Morgan knew it probably meant she disapproved of the segment. He swallowed hard and decided to face her head-on, to get it over with. He figured eventually her opinion would make its way back to him. He'd rather hear it straight from the boss than have it filtered through layers of cops with their own agendas. To Morgan's surprise, she broached the topic immediately.

"She said, 'I had to hold my breath when they asked you that question about why hasn't the case been proceeding, why hasn't somebody been charged?' She said, 'I saw that little snicker on your face when you leaned back in the chair and made that comment about we're continuing to work with the D.A.'s office.' She said, 'That was the best thing you could say,'" Morgan recalls with relief.

Chief Jane Perlov was not a person who freely gave compliments, especially not to Chris Morgan. It was no secret that the two strong personalities had locked horns on several occasions. Morgan felt like her reaction to the show was about as close as he was going to get to an "atta-boy," and he gratefully accepted it.

BURNING BRIDGES

At this point in the investigation Morgan realized he had probably taken too many risks and burned too many bridges. He and Tom Ford were now on opposite sides of a raging river without even so much as a stray log to bridge the ever-widening gap. Morgan had a lot of animosity toward Ford for not having moved forward with what Morgan had felt was a very viable case. He knew that his own actions, going around Ford to Howard Cummings and Colon Willoughby, would forever cast him as a troublemaker in Ford's eyes, but he just didn't care anymore. It wasn't something he could afford to waste precious energy worrying about.

While Morgan continued to wait for the North Carolina Supreme Court to make its decision, life and death went on in Raleigh. Murders continued to happen, murders that needed Morgan's attention.

Around this same time Chief Perlov was working on decentralizing the investigative unit. The idea was to have detectives in each district investigating crimes in that district instead of having them all based out of headquarters. The other objective of Perlov's plan was to concentrate more on quality-of-life crimes, such as petty theft or car break-ins, which affected the largest number of people. By comparison, there were only a small number of murders every year, and thus they affected a relatively small number of people. This philosophy irked Morgan to his core. In his mind there is no greater crime than murder, and in his opinion, murders clearly affect people much more deeply than the theft of a bike or stereo. There was no comparison.

To Morgan, this new agenda meant fewer resources would be allocated toward murder investigations. Because each district would have just a handful of detectives to investigate its own crimes, there would no longer be a large team of detectives at the central office handling every homicide.

"Let the damn car break-ins, stuff like that, fall by the wayside. When somebody takes a life, it can never be replaced," says Morgan disgustedly. "My heart and my time will still largely be focused on people's whose lives have been stolen."

But the decentralization was going to happen whether Morgan liked it or not.

BUMPER DEATH NOTIFICATION

Fifty-five-year-old Robert Sanchez Saiz was a Raleigh Public Utilities worker who'd been robbed at gunpoint and killed in the winter of 2002. A group of robbers burst into the break room and demanded everyone's wallet. Saiz tried to slip out the back door and was shot. Many hours after Morgan and his detectives started working the case, he realized that no one had notified Saiz's wife, Debra, that her husband was dead. Morgan decided he would go with Detective Amy Russo to Cary, a suburb of Raleigh, where the man had lived with his family, and break the awful news himself.

Over the years Morgan had taken on the nickname "Bump" or "Bumper" after a character in Joe Wambaugh's book *The Blue Knight*. A fellow cop dubbed Morgan "Bump" in the late 1970s because the real name of the character in the book was William Morgan (Chris Morgan's full name is William Christopher Morgan). Like Chris Morgan, William Morgan was a large cop with an even bigger personality. As nicknames have a way of doing, this one stuck like glue to Morgan. Cops got so used to calling Morgan "Bump" that some didn't even know his real name. He accepted the moniker with humility and just a smidgen of pride on account of the fact that his colleagues had bothered to name him after a colorful character torn right out of a classic tale.

It was a cold November night when Morgan and Russo headed to Saiz's home. Morgan slipped on his best white felt fedora and his overcoat as he got out of the car. He and Russo walked solemnly to the door of the apartment and knocked. It wasn't the first time Morgan had made a "death knock," but it was the first time in a long while. A slight Hispanic woman in a robe answered the door. It was Debra Saiz, Robert Saiz's widow.

"Immediately she broke down and said, 'Oh my God, he's died, he's dead,' before we ever said one word," Morgan says, sounding somewhat stunned as he recalled the woman's reaction. "From that point on, me going to the front door in a hat became known as a 'Bumper Death Notification.' "

Morgan had become so well known as the detective in the hat on television who investigated murders that his mere presence was enough to let someone know a loved one had died. It was an unexpected side effect of his new-found fame, and one he wasn't sure he liked.

SHIRLEY LANG

On Wednesday, January 29, 2003, the body of a forty-four-year-old nursing student was found on the grounds of the Dorothea Dix Hospital, a local public mental institution. A cop on foot, chasing a suspect who had committed an unrelated assault with a machete, practically stumbled over Shirley Lang's body in the woods just off a path on the edge of the property. While the body had no connection to the assault, the officer called it in on his radio. When Morgan arrived at the scene, he was appalled by the sight of Lang's body, and equally amazed that at this point in his career anything could still appall him.

"It was a brutal murder. She was cut and slashed repeatedly about the head, and neck, and face. It showed a lot of emotion. It was one of the first things that stuck with me in that case," says Morgan, shaking his head.

Morgan strongly believes that in order to get close enough to cut someone with a knife, to kill someone in such a savage way, you have to know the person. A stranger doesn't want to have any physical connection to someone's death, which is why strangers generally use guns and stay farther away from their victims. But rage, rage came from a deep dark place that was inextricably entwined with the killer's relationship to the victim.

Lang had been partially disrobed, and she'd had a tree branch forced down her throat. The scene made Morgan sick to his stomach, and at the same time even more determined to find Shirley Lang's killer.

And like every other case by that point, he looked at it in the context of Eric Miller. These days Eric Miller's case was the lens that every new case passed through.

"It seemed like every case I got, every new case that came in, I somehow ended up comparing it to Eric Miller. Eric was fast becoming the focal point of my life," Morgan admits. "It was kind of like the anchor I was holding on to."

What if Eric's killer had left clues as Shirley Lang's killer had done? What if Eric's killer had been sloppy and emotional? But none of these what-ifs would do him any good now. In contrast to Shirley Lang's murder, Eric's death was cold, sterile, without obvious traces of emotion. Eric's killer had managed to cover her tracks. There was no crime scene to speak of where detectives could have gathered clear forensic evidence.

In Shirley Lang's case, Morgan expected justice to be much more swift. He dove into it headfirst hoping to get some immediate gratification in a way he couldn't get from the languishing Miller case. Shirley Lang had been a hardworking, churchgoing woman who'd been missing for three days. Besides having raised two children, Lang was a nursing student at Wake Technical Community College and an intern at the Dorothea Dix Hospital, a state psychiatric facility. Her husband, fifty-five-year-old Daniel Lang, had not reported her missing until she had been gone for thirty-six hours. Yet when he was interviewed by police, he showed no concern about the fact that his wife was gone, that she had missed church, that friends had been asking questions. It didn't take a seasoned investigator to realize that Daniel Lang was hiding something. Yet Lang appeared to be as little concerned about the perception that he might be involved in a murder as he was about his wife's disappearance and her death.

"Just as Ann Miller should have been much more concerned than she was when she first heard the words *arsenic poisoning*," Morgan says, wondering how killers can think they are going to get away with their crimes when their culpability is so obvious.

Again, Morgan lived by the adage that "the truth makes sense, and if it doesn't make sense, it isn't the truth." Morgan hadn't come up with this belief by accident—it was part experience, part history. He read about a medieval mathematician named Occam who preached that in the absence of overwhelming evidence to the contrary, the simplest solution is almost always the right solution. Morgan took this theory to heart.

Morgan took over in the interrogation room that night with Daniel Lang, not because his detectives weren't doing a good job, but because he knew the truth, and he wanted Daniel Lang to *know* that he knew the truth. It was something he needed to do, for himself, and for Shirley Lang, and even in some small way that he did not completely understand, for Eric.

" 'You tell me the truth, you can go home. You don't tell me the truth, we're going to have a big problem, Daniel,' "

Morgan recalls saying to Lang. "I decided, 'Daniel Lang, you're not leaving my police station unless it's in handcuffs.'"

They went around and around in circles, covering the same ground over and over again. Nothing made sense. Morgan knew this was his only chance, that if he waited even one day, Daniel Lang would get an attorney and the conversation would be over, just as it had been over with Ann Miller after that very first night at the Raleigh Police Station, just as it had been over with Derril Willard the day they searched his home.

Finally, after about two hours, Morgan got in Lang's face. "I said, 'Daniel, I think you killed your wife and I want you to tell me something that will prove me wrong,'" Morgan says through gritted teeth, imitating his tone that night.

And then the unthinkable happened. The circling became real instead of just metaphorical. Both men stood up and started rounding the table like wild animals readying for attack. Lang was a slight man, about 160 pounds, and Morgan weighed about a hundred pounds more than that. But Lang was obviously not deterred by Morgan's formidable size. Suddenly he pounced, jumping across the table in an attempt to head-butt Morgan, but like a cartoon character, he literally bounced off Morgan's large frame and fell backward. Morgan recalls it being almost comical. After a brief struggle between the two men, detectives waiting in the hallway ran into the room and subdued Lang. He was charged with assaulting an officer and placed under a one million dollar bond. It wasn't a murder charge, but it was enough to keep him behind bars until they could make a case. Lang's head butt turned out to be just what investigators needed to buy some time.

The next day Morgan sent one of his detectives, Mary Blalock, to the North Carolina Medical Examiner's Office in Chapel Hill to observe Shirley Lang's autopsy. Meanwhile, he was looking for anything short of a confession that would make a murder charge stick to Daniel Lang. He didn't have to wait long.

Blalock called Morgan from the medical examiner's office and told him that a note had been found stuffed down in Shirley Lang's pants, and it appeared to have been written by her. Morgan could hear Blalock smoothing out the crumpled paper in the background as she prepared to read the note.

"The note said: 'My husband and a man is trying to kill me, help.' It was signed 'Shirley Lang.' That's something that doesn't happen every day," Morgan says. "I've often wondered how many murder victims know the person responsible for their death. Eric, despite all of his good qualities and his high level of intelligence, was simply unable to comprehend *who* was trying to kill him."

The note raised one troubling issue, however. Who was "the man" Shirley referred to in the note? Morgan said his squad spent days trying to find the other person who might have helped Daniel Lang kill his wife.

What they uncovered was that Daniel Lang, who was himself a nurse at the mental hospital, had been intimate with several patients, including a woman who had killed her children with a hammer and then set their house on fire. There was a dirty old mattress in the woods near where Shirley Lang's body had been found where the patient said she and Daniel Lang had had sex. Morgan describes the woman as rather "manly," and he always wondered if Shirley—in what must have been her traumatic dying moments—had mistaken the patient for a man; but for all of their countless hours of investigation, detectives could never determine for certain if there was anyone else involved in the murder.

The note was still enough, however, to convince Daniel Lang's attorney, Johnny Gaskins, that his client should plead guilty. Lang was also charged with a first-degree sex offense against another mentally ill patient. The woman in that case had decapitated her three-year-old son and put his body in a closet in Fayetteville, North Carolina. It had been decided that she was not competent to stand trial, and so she'd been sent to Dorothea Dix Hospital, where she subsequently met Daniel Lang and became sexually involved with him.

While nothing surprised Morgan after so many years as a cop, he still couldn't understand how people could be so cruel. Truth be told, he didn't want to understand. If he ever did, it would mean he had something in common with them. The day he started understanding this was the day he needed to hang up his white fedora.

Ultimately, Daniel Lang was allowed to plead guilty to second-degree murder because he had prostate cancer and was not expected to live long (Lang died in prison on

December 27, 2006). Morgan didn't care what sentence Lang got, as long as he was never on the street again. But Ann Miller *was* still on the street, and Morgan was convinced now more than ever that she was a dangerous person. In Shirley Lang, Morgan saw Eric Miller, and every other innocent victim. He was reminded that he still had a lot of work to do.

"Their lives had all been ended by someone who thought they had the right to kill, to take that life before it was fully realized," says Morgan angrily.

STRANGER THAN FICTION

Prior to Eric Miller's death, the last recorded arsenic homicide in North Carolina was that of a turkey farmer named Dorian Lanier on November 19, 1997. He died in a rural part of North Carolina at Duplin County Hospital in Kenansville. The poisoning was discovered when Dr. Corbett Quinn, the Duplin County medical examiner, performed an autopsy and found that Lanier had toxic levels of arsenic in his body. After a prolonged investigation, Lanier's wife, forty-five-year-old Pamela Sanders Williams Lanier, was charged with her husband's murder and arrested on January 5, 1999. It was also discovered that she had had a previous husband who had died some years earlier under suspicious circumstances, although she was never charged in connection with his death. He'd been a strong swimmer, yet had drowned in only three feet of water while checking his crab pots along the coast.

Because real life truly *is* stranger than fiction, it turned out that one of Dorian Lanier's sisters just happened to live directly across the street from Ann Miller's rental home in Wilmington. Another one of Lanier's sisters contacted the Millers to offer her sympathy, saying that her family understood their ordeal and the suffering their son had gone through.

Lanier's sister, who lived across farm Ann, joked about getting a petition up to throw her out of the neighborhood. But besides sympathy, she had one important thing she could offer the case: she agreed to keep tabs on Ann and tell the Millers anything they wanted to know about her comings and goings.

"Fate brought these two families together who had endured so much of the same heartaches. The main consistency—their [Ann and Pamela's] ability to do these horrible things, to sit and watch somebody die a slow lingering death at their own hands," Morgan says.

In many ways Morgan thought Dorian Lanier's death was even more horrific than Eric Miller's, because Lanier never sought medical help until the end. He was a good old boy, a farmer, and was skeptical about doctors. It pained Morgan to find out that close to the end of Dorian's life, Pamela Lanier had merely put a plastic tarp on her husband's bed because he could not control his vomiting or his bowels. At least as an educated man, a scientist, Eric had realized that he needed *some* medical intervention.

In Dorian Lanier's case, prosecutors had finally been able to convict Pamela Lanier. She received a life sentence in prison, something the Millers could only dream about at this point for Ann.

SHOULD I STAY OR SHOULD I GO?

Morgan felt like he was growing old waiting for the North Carolina Supreme Court to make a decision. The case was practically at a standstill, hinging on the legal issue of attorney-client privilege. And Morgan was painfully aware that this one small piece of evidence from Rick Gammon still might or might not crack the case wide open.

"I can't arrest her. It became a situation of almost total frustration for me. I've never been very good at waiting," Morgan admits, as if that might not already be obvious.

While he waited, Morgan began to notice that his colleagues, the guys he had gone through the police academy with, the guys he had patrolled the streets of Raleigh with for years, were starting to retire. In North Carolina cops must put in thirty years before they can retire with full benefits. With stored sick leave and vacation time, Morgan knew he had enough to follow his peers on their journey to a simpler life, but the truth was, he wasn't ready to go. He had unfinished business. It had always been like this. Every time Morgan even *considered* retirement, there was always a case that pulled him back.

"The commitment I made was that Ann Miller was going to be locked up prior to me ever retiring," Morgan says firmly.

COLLEGE DAYS

August 22, 2003, was the one Friday that Morgan had a family commitment. It was the one Friday morning that he would not be able to check the computer the minute the North Carolina Supreme Court handed down its most recent decisions. But the commitment was too important to miss. One of his twin daughters, Laura, was starting her freshman year at East Carolina University in Greenville, North Carolina, and Daddy needed to help her move into her dorm room. *Surely,* Morgan thought, *the Supreme Court wouldn't pick the last Friday in August to make this momentous decision in the Ann Miller case?* But of course, just like the traffic jam that always happens when you're late for an important meeting, it turned out to be the day.

While he was on the road to Greenville, Morgan got a call from Verus Miller on his cell phone telling him that a decision had been made. In his heart Morgan felt like *he* was the one who should have been calling Verus, not the other way around. But life gets in the way of work, and work gets in the way of life. Quickly, Morgan cast off his guilt about not sitting diligently by his computer that morning and he started calling around to get more details about the decision. He found out that the court had handed down a very narrow order compelling Rick Gammon to tell Superior Court judge Donald Stephens what he knew in chambers. Stephens would then decide what part of the information, if any, investigators were entitled to. Under the court's ruling, anything that Derril Willard told Gammon about a third party (presumably Ann Miller) that did not incriminate him (Willard) was fair game and did not violate attorney-client privilege.

"It's almost exclusive to this particular case. Nobody's rights were ever going to be disturbed, interrupted, lessened by what was written in that decision," Morgan explains. "They didn't like the idea of monkeying with attorney-client privilege any more than the law professors did, but they did the right thing for Eric Miller."

As soon as the decision came down, the media went on a feeding frenzy, calling Morgan on his cell phone all day long. But he didn't let it stop him with his most important task of the day—helping his daughter.

"I'd be moving another footlocker, or box of college-girl stuff, from the parking lot to the dorm, and it would ring again." Morgan chuckles. He had a pat response for every caller. " 'We feel very encouraged by this. We're still seeking truth and justice for Eric Miller. We've come this far and we keep going further and further, it can't stop now.' "

Morgan knew this was an important legal step toward his goal of seeing Ann Miller locked up forever. For the first time in a long while he felt like he might even live to see it happen.

He also knew Judge Stephens well enough to be sure that he wouldn't order Gammon to turn this information over unless he thought it might solve the case. Morgan still didn't know what Gammon had, but he figured it had to be important. In his wildest dreams he could not have imagined just how important it would turn out to be.

WEDDING BELLS

Judge Stephens reviewed Gammon's affidavit and ordered him to hand over the information to investigators on October 2, 2003. As predicted, Rick Gammon appealed and once again the case came to a grinding halt while Morgan and the Miller family waited for the North Carolina Supreme Court to hear the appeal.

The euphoria of the original Supreme Court decision was starting to wear off when Morgan found out that Ann Miller's family was "circling the wagons." First he learned that Dan and Nancy Brier had moved to Wilmington in the spring of 2003 to be closer to Ann and Clare. Then, on November 29, 2003, the Reverend Raymond Shepley married Ann Miller and Paul Kontz at the North Wilmington Community Church, of which they were members. Paul Kontz was the man investigators had seen with Ann during their intense surveillance of her. He was the electrician, the Christian rock musician, the man whose house she had spent eight hours holed up in while Morgan parked his big butt in an oleander bush.

Morgan also found out that Ann had bought a home in Wilmington where she, Clare, Paul, and Paul's daughter were living. How had she managed to afford a nice brick house in a quiet suburban neighborhood? Morgan learned that she had been hired by another pharmaceutical company called PPD. It amazed him that while the highest court in the state was determining Ann's fate, she was dusting off her résumé, investing in real estate, and taking another trip down the aisle. But then again there was one thing Morgan knew for sure about Ann—she was good at denial. *Very good*.

SECOND THOUGHTS

Even a tough guy like Morgan was not immune to pressure. Suddenly things were starting to pile up. Almost every day his friend and colleague Captain Ken Mathias was coming into Morgan's office and asking when he was going to retire. The truth was Mathias wasn't asking because *he* wanted to know; he was asking because *Chief Perlov* wanted to know. Morgan felt like Perlov was ready to send him out to pasture. Morgan was the kind of employee who simply stirred the pot too much, and he assumed that she saw him as an old-school cop who didn't embrace her progressive ways. It was very unlikely that this impasse between two strong-willed people was ever going to be bridged.

Morgan tried not to let it get to him, but it did. According to him, the tension between himself and the chief worsened when she accused his unit of failing to find and arrest a man on an accessory-to-murder charge. Morgan recalls that his colleagues were aghast when he challenged Chief Perlov's accusations in a meeting in front of everyone. Two detectives were making gestures at him to "stop already." One had his hand on his throat; the other was covering his mouth with one hand and making a "cut" sign across his neck with the other. But Morgan couldn't help himself; he was hot and everyone, including the chief, knew it.

"It ticked me off," Morgan says.

And then, in early 2004, as if he was not under enough pressure, Morgan's eighty-year-old mother came down with kidney cancer. Again, life was throwing him a curveball, getting in the way of work, as work had gotten in the way of Morgan's life so many times before.

"My mother had been such a definite and great influence to me, as well as my best friend, that it was devastating news to me," says Morgan, choking back tears.

The idea of retirement started to surface again, and this time seemed like a logical step. Clearly, the brass wanted Morgan out. And clearly, Morgan had an obligation to be there for his mother as she had been there for him throughout every moment of his life.

"Thirty years of being a police officer is long enough for almost anybody," Morgan says. "But up until that point and time, the only thing that had occupied my future was seeing Ann Miller go to jail for killing her husband . . . I hadn't stayed for the benefit of the Raleigh Police Department. I stayed for the benefit of Verus Miller and the rest of the Miller family."

Morgan was torn by his desire to stay and solve the case, and his need to move on. He'd always had a hard-to-kick habit of getting closer than he should to the families of murder victims. It had happened with the Millers; it had happened with the Bennetts. He was fully aware of the problem yet powerless to do anything about it. This made it even harder to leave.

"I got close to them because they needed it, and I needed it," Morgan admits. "What I think they got from me [was] they always knew who to call."

But ultimately, common sense won out. Morgan knew that he had stayed at the party way too long, longer than most people. It was truly time to go. He wasn't sure what was on the other side of the mountaintop, but he was sure looking forward to finding out. Now that District Attorney Colon Willoughby had won the case in the North Carolina Supreme Court, Morgan was confident that Ann Miller would eventually be brought to justice. This meant he could leave knowing that he had done his job.

But before he could walk out the door, Morgan had to do one more thing. He had to tell the families who depended upon him to solve their loved ones' murders that he would no longer be their point of contact, *their* detective.

Verus Miller was disappointed, but not shocked. Morgan told him that the wheels were in motion now to solve the case, and that it would happen with or without him. Morgan recalled that Verus bravely and graciously accepted the news of his retirement. He expected nothing less from the man whom he had grown to know as a salt-of-the-earth stand-up guy over the years. In short, Morgan considered Verus Miller to be a class act all the way, and he admired the incredible strength that Verus had shown throughout the entire investigation.

But telling Carmon Bennett, Stephanie Bennett's father, was another story. Morgan dreaded it, almost as much as he dreaded making a death notification to a family. Unlike the Miller case, there was no suspect in Stephanie Bennett's murder. Unlike the Miller family, the Bennetts had no expectation of justice in the near future. Morgan felt like he was leaving them empty-handed after he had promised them he would be there until the end.

Because he knew how devastating the news would be to Carmon Bennett, Morgan decided to tell him about his pending retirement in person. He took a trip to Roanoke, Virginia, the small town where Stephanie grew up, several hours north of Raleigh. He brought along the detectives who were going to take over the case to show Carmon that the investigation would continue.

"[Carmon Bennett] had reached a point of desperation and was still circling desperation daily," recalls Morgan, "because we still had absolutely no idea who was responsible for the murder of his daughter. He had tears in both eyes, and I think I did, too, because our relationship, while it would remain a good relationship between good friends . . . it was taking a turn that I don't think either one of us really wanted."

Sergeant Clem Perry and Detective Ken Copeland would be taking over the case when Morgan left. Carmon Bennett welcomed them and accepted Morgan's glowing review of their skills despite his skepticism. In hindsight Morgan credits himself for picking Copeland to lead the charge. Called the "garbage man," Copeland was known for picking up every piece of evidence, no matter how trivial it seemed, and examining it thoroughly. Ultimately, years later, Copeland, along with another bright detective, Jackie Taylor, would be able to do what Morgan hadn't—catch Stephanie Bennett's killer.

It was done. Morgan was leaving. The paperwork was

in. The retirement parties were under way, one after another. He was roasted. People told stories about "Bump." He got gifts, cakes, and plaques with his name on them. Finally, he was ready to go.

When Gammon's appeal was denied by the North Carolina Supreme Court on May 7, 2004, all Morgan could do was smile. The dominoes were in place. They were falling in the right direction on a smooth path to justice. Now he could sit back in his worn recliner and watch them land from the comfort of his own home.

"I was waiting for Perlov to ask me to stay and then I could leave with a clear conscience," Morgan jokes.

Be careful what you wish for.

DELIVERANCE

On May 27, 2004, Rick Gammon delivered a small white envelope to Colon Willoughby. It contained one single sheet of paper. It was the information that Gammon had been ordered to turn over based on the very narrow ruling handed down by the North Carolina Supreme Court.

Because of the extreme sensitivity of the information, Gammon chose to hand-deliver the envelope to the Wake County District Attorney's Office. The media created a circuslike atmosphere, following Gammon from his office across the pedestrian mall into the Wake County Courthouse. They piled into the elevator with him and jockeyed to get closer to the white envelope in his hand, as if they might be able to see its contents with their X-ray vision. Gammon, no stranger to media attention, smiled coyly as reporters threw out questions at him that he politely refused to answer.

After Gammon entered the Wake County District Attorney's Office, he handed the envelope to Colon Willoughby. Willoughby had assembled his team of prosecutors in his office, as well as investigators, including Morgan, for the big event. Morgan remembers that before Gammon turned to leave, he flashed everyone his trademark wry smile as if to say: "Have at it!"

Willoughby immediately handed the envelope to Morgan. Morgan then read what would come to be known in the media as "paragraph 12" and in court as "Exhibit A". It was the one paragraph of Gammon's long affidavit that Judge Donald Stephens said must be released. In line with the Supreme Court's order, it indicted Ann Miller in Eric Miller's death, but it did not incriminate Derril Willard. It fit the very narrow standard the justices had outlined in their ruling.

One thing it didn't fit, however, was anyone's speculation or expectations about what it would contain. No one, including Morgan, had expected the information to be so direct and so damning to Ann Miller.

The actual text of paragraph 12 reads as follows:

Mr. Willard then stated that on one recent occasion he had met Mrs. Miller in a parking lot, and they had a conversation while in an SUV. He stated that during his conversation Mrs. Miller was crying and that she told him she had been to the hospital where Mr. Miller had been admitted. She stated to Mr. Willard that she was by herself in the room with Mr. Miller for a period of time. She then told Mr. Willard that she took a syringe and needle from her purse and injected the contents of the syringe into Mr. Miller's IV. Upon being questioned as to the contents of the syringe, Mr. Willard either stated that the substance was from work, or that Mrs. Miller told him it was from work. He then stated that he asked Mrs. Miller why she had done this, and she replied, "I don't know." Mr. Willard surmised that Mrs. Miller was attempting to end Mr. Miller's suffering from his illness with these actions. Although Mr. Gammon and Mr. Fitzhugh do not recall specifically whether Mr. Willard or Mrs. Miller used the word "arsenic" with reference to the contents of the syringe, it was clear that the substance contained in the syringe was poisonous. Mr. Willard then stated he knew nothing further of the circumstances surrounding Eric Miller's death. He also stated that he had not told anyone including his wife, about Mrs. Miller's statements to him.

There was no date on the document stating when this gruesome incident took place, but Morgan had one in mind. On the evening of November 19, 2000, during Eric Miller's first hospital stay at Rex, his condition had started to deteriorate again after he had showed signs of improving. That night the on-call physician wrote in his chart that he didn't expect Eric to make it through the night because his symptoms had worsened. This was the same day that a heavy-metals test had been ordered on Eric. The results hadn't come in yet, but Morgan wondered, had Ann *known* they might be onto her? Did she overhear someone talking about the test? Had she gotten nervous and tried to end Eric's life once and for all?

"Something had to happen to send this kid downhill like he went. I think that likely as not that was the night that Ann, as described in paragraph twelve, comes in there and juices him with arsenic one more time, trying to get this over with," Morgan says with disgust.

This theory was one that ultimately gelled and became bedrock of the investigation, although it was almost derailed by a well-meaning nurse. Nurse Charlene Blaine reported seeing a man who looked like Derril Willard enter Eric Miller's room on the night of November 19. This was a problem, a big problem. This smacked of reasonable doubt, because if Willard had been there, then conceivably *he* could have given Eric poison in his IV instead of Ann. Yet there was no indication from anyone else, including the hospital's visitor log, that Willard had ever been there. But Blaine was convinced.

Then Morgan had an epiphany. He realized that Blaine was identifying Willard from the picture of him that had been widely circulated on television, his high school graduation picture. Willard the grown man looked nothing like his former boyish self. Morgan realized that Nurse Blaine had probably mistaken one of Eric's sisters' husbands for Willard. After sharing pictures of the men with her, Blaine positively identified the brother-in-law as the man who had visited Eric's room that night, *not* Derril Willard. The train was back on track.

Paragraph 12 was not what Morgan had expected, but it

was exactly what he needed. It was the piece of the puzzle Colon Willoughby needed to convict Ann Miller in front of a jury of her peers. It was the final piece of evidence Morgan needed to allow him to retire with a clear conscience.

"I realized at that point that Ann Miller was going to go to jail for the murder of her husband," Morgan says with a smile.

A NEW SHERIFF IN TOWN

Morgan heard her coming down the hall before he saw her. He could hear her high heels clicking on the linoleum and her pleasant, even voice as she said hello to people she passed. His heart skipped a beat not because this was the woman of his dreams, but because she was the *prosecutor* of his dreams.

Morgan felt as if Assistant District Attorney Becky Holt had ridden into his office on a white horse to save the Eric Miller case.

"She said, 'I'm up here on the Miller case.' I said, 'That's Ford's case.' She said, 'Not anymore,' " Morgan recalls with sheer exuberance in his voice.

Morgan couldn't conceal his excitement. He liked and respected Holt very much and considered her to be a cops' prosecutor. She was someone who valued the opinions of investigators and treated them as part of the prosecution team. She also informed him that Assistant District Attorney Doug Faucette would help her prosecute the case. Morgan viewed Faucette, who "looked like the boy who mowed my lawn," as one of the brightest young stars in the district attorney's office.

"At that point I was saying, 'Ann Miller, you don't know what's happened to you, girl, and you're fixing to go down,'" Morgan states with vengefulness.

HELL FREEZES OVER

All of a sudden Morgan was having second thoughts again about his retirement. He knew that paragraph 12 would help Becky Holt take the case to the grand jury and that she would no doubt get an indictment, but he worried about what would happen after that. How would she prepare for a trial based on a four-year investigation without the help of the lead investigator?

"I was really torn," says Morgan.

But he had made a decision, a very difficult decision, and he intended to stick with it. His last day on the job, May 31, 2004, started like any other day, except for the boxes stacked up in the corner of his office. His colleagues came in to say their good-byes and spend one more afternoon in his office talking junk. They traded stories and jabs. It felt good to know that he had developed such close relationships with his cop friends over the years. He would miss them, but he knew he would see them again. Morgan kept telling himself that this wasn't an ending, but a beginning to a whole new chapter in his life, even if he didn't know exactly where it would lead.

Then Morgan got the call. It was Chief Perlov's secretary,

Pat Bridgers. She asked Morgan if he would be in his office because the chief wanted to pay him a little visit. Without hesitation, Morgan said he would be there and told her to come on down. He assumed Perlov was making a very generous gesture to come by and say farewell, to smooth over any rough patches they had experienced in their short tenure together. He actually thought it was very big of her. It was something he hadn't expected, but something that he would accept humbly and with sincere appreciation.

But Morgan could never have imagined what happened next. Chief Perlov, all business, entered Morgan's office and sat down in a chair directly across from his desk. She nodded briefly to the other officers congregated in Morgan's office and then turned her gaze to Morgan.

She told him that Colon Willoughby had paid her a visit and relayed that Ann Miller was going to be indicted. She also told him that Willoughby wanted Morgan to stay with the Raleigh Police Department just a little bit longer in order to help the prosecution team put the case together.

"I said, 'Chief, are you asking me to stay?'" Morgan remembers asking coyly. "She said, 'Yes, this is important.'"

Morgan says Captain Ken Mathias's jaw literally dropped to the ground. The other officers looked just as shell-shocked. Two rivals who were worthy of a comic-book story line had made nice in the interest of justice. It was almost too much for Morgan to take in. It felt better than he ever could have imagined in his wildest dreams. It was like the Sally Fields moment at the Oscars—*you like me,* he thought incredulously, *you really like me?*

"By the next day I was back, [a] sworn, never-retired, Raleigh Police officer," says Morgan.

GAME ON

Morgan jumped head-on into the task of preparing the case. He began the tedious process of bringing prosecutors up-to-date on four years' worth of work. It was painstaking, time-consuming, detail work, but Morgan was reinvigorated.

"I was literally floating through the next several months because I knew that the end was in sight," Morgan recalls. "I was finally going to retire in comfort with the knowledge that Ann Miller was going to be in jail where she belongs. That sustained me."

Morgan had always loved his work. It was never a chore for him, it was something that defined him as much as his family did. But this chapter in his career was the culmination of everything that had come before. It symbolized the success of a long, hard-fought battle to find justice for Eric Miller. It was a fight Morgan had never given up on, but one he'd often wondered if he would win.

While Morgan and prosecutors were busy preparing their case, one of Ann Miller's attorneys, Joe Cheshire, was busy doing damage control. As long as Morgan had known Cheshire, he'd been a defense attorney with no problem about coming out in public and proclaiming his clients' innocence. The handsome southern attorney with his shock of curly hair, goatee, and wire-framed glasses had a way of wearing his righteous indignation on his sleeve without alienating people. When Joe Cheshire said his client was innocent, people believed him, even Chris Morgan. Above everything else, Joe Cheshire had integrity.

"If he's got a client that he actually thinks is innocent, he's going to be out front in the face, all over the media, telling everybody who will listen to him that, 'Hey world, my guy didn't do it, he's innocent.' I mean Joe's not a bit bashful about coming out and making those kinds of statements," Morgan says.

Morgan noticed right away that Cheshire didn't say Ann Miller was innocent in media interviews. He said things like she was "sad over the death of her husband," "has very strong faith," and "believes the truth will come out." It made Morgan curious. And it made him wonder what Ann Miller had told Joe Cheshire.

NINE

There are tones of voice
that mean more than words.
—ROBERT FROST

Morgan moved into a special role, where he was just working on the Miller case, and Lieutenant John Lynch took over the homicide unit. Immediately, this created friction within the department because Lynch and Morgan had decidedly different management styles. Lynch was a straightforward cop, a traditional investigator who got results through good old-fashioned police work. Morgan, on the other hand, had always marched to a slightly different beat.

Even though by the summer of 2004, Lynch was technically in charge of the homicide investigators, Morgan says detectives continued coming to him for advice, playing the two men off each other.

The situation intensified Morgan's desire to finish his business on the Miller case and get on with his retirement and the rest of his life.

"The time was coming when I was going to have to get out of there [both] for my own personal well-being and so the police department could carry on with their own very important work," Morgan says.

EVIL WAYS

Morgan can talk for days about the motivation behind the criminal mind. In fact, if you don't interrupt him and just let him go, chances are he will. He believes that most people, including investigators, expect a motive that is logical. But Morgan contends that the problem with this expectation is that there are certain kinds of criminals motivated by something that no ordinary person can truly understand—*evil*.

In the Miller case no one could truly grasp Ann Miller's particular motive for killing her husband. According to Morgan, prosecutors Becky Holt and Doug Faucette were having a tough time with this. Like anyone getting ready to try a case, they wanted it to be something clear and definite that they could explain to a jury. Was it another man (or men), was it money, was it the fear of losing her child?

"She didn't want Eric around as an ex-husband. She just wanted Eric gone," Morgan says with conviction. "In order to fully understand Ann Miller and her motivations, you have to believe in the worst kind of perceptible evil that there is in the world. The worst evil in the world is the evil that exists in the minds of a psychopathic personality because it has no necessary rhyme or reason attached to it.

Psychopaths, we know, exist only to provide and to further their own wants and desires. They have no compassion, they have no empathy, and they have no concern with anybody other than themselves, and that's where the crux of Ann Miller's motive and therefore her evil come from."

Again, unlike conditions that psychologists term as "mental illness," psychopathy is not a definable mental illness per se, but a group of behaviors associated certain personality disorders. Often people who exhibit these behaviors are still very high-functioning in society and, therefore, give no clear indication that there's anything wrong with them.

Morgan believes that for Ann Miller, risk taking was like a drug addiction. It was a thrill she couldn't resist. In fact, he feels her obsession with taking risks was the only thing in her life that she was powerless to conquer. For example, Ann's pattern of affairs, blatant affairs involving trips, frequent phone calls, and steamy e-mails; with each man, Morgan thought, Ann grew bolder and more cavalier in her belief that she would never get caught. He believes Ann's plot to kill her husband was born directly out of that personality trait; a desire to push the envelope, to see just how far she could take it.

"[Psychopaths are] not drooling trolls that live under a bridge. Most of them are well integrated into society. Most of them are neighbors, coworkers, friends," Morgan explains.

Verus Miller, Eric's father, recommended a book to Morgan called *People of the Lie* by M. Scott Peck. It talks about psychopaths' ability to mimic proper social behavior while staying focused on their only goal, pleasing themselves at any cost. Morgan read it and began to see major parallels between its subject and Ann Miller. He picked up a copy for Becky Holt at a used-book store at the beach and urged her to read it as well.

Morgan sees Ann as someone who "played the role" of the devoted wife, as evidenced by her involvement in the couples-counseling class at church. He sees her as someone who "played the role" of a devoted mother, even though in the midst of her quest to get pregnant, she was having an affair with Carl Mackewicz. He also sees her as someone who "played the role" of a dedicated scientist, while her colleagues said she was more interested in attracting men in the office than paying attention to her work.

Morgan believes all people have the potential to kill if sufficiently driven by anger or rage. But the difference with psychopaths is that they need no anger. He or she simply perceives that the victim is standing in the way of what he or she wants, and therefore that person must be removed. And the psychopath experiences no remorse, while the rage killer may be haunted or even internally tortured forever by what he or she has done.

Morgan feels Ann Miller was without rage or remorse because she was and is a psychopath. But it was a hard pill for others, including the prosecutors, to swallow. He had been living with her in his head for four years. They were just getting to know her.

"Most of the people who knew Ann Miller would have described her in any way other than being a psychopath," concedes Morgan.

Everyone wanted there to be something else—the suspicious death of a previous boyfriend maybe—but there was no evidence that Ann had killed before. Morgan believes Ann, like other psychopaths, was motivated by the specific opportunity of the situation, and he speculated that she probably wouldn't kill again unless she was backed into the same dusty corner of her life.

MAKING NICE

Morgan had officially set his new retirement date for September 1, 2004. He felt like it was in the interest of justice for him to "bug out" of the Raleigh Police Department once and for all. He would still be around to help with the case, just not on the official payroll. Not being paid had never stopped him from working before, and it certainly wouldn't make a difference now that the Ann Miller conviction train had left the station. He would be on it paycheck or no paycheck.

But before Morgan left, he had some unfinished business to deal with—namely Dr. Thomas Clark from the medical examiner's office.

Morgan had not spoken with Dr. Clark in any depth since their tense meeting in the spring of 2001 when the autopsy report was released. But the ego clashing that had gone on between Clark and the original prosecutor, Tom Ford, did not bode well in Morgan's mind for Clark's relationship with the new prosecution team.

Becky Holt also knew that Dr. Clark was going to be a

key witness, and she had to have him on her side. So she asked Morgan to set up a meeting between Clark and the prosecution team in August 2004.

Easier said than done—it took a while for Morgan (a phone person) to get through to Dr. Clark (an e-mail person). When they finally connected, Morgan recalls Clark told him he had nothing to add to the case, that his autopsy report was complete, and that he was a busy man with no time for a meeting. But Morgan pleaded with him, saying that it was necessary to update the new prosecutors on the case. He confided that the case was finally going before a grand jury and they needed to get ready for trial, and Clark begrudgingly agreed to a meeting.

It was a meeting that Morgan would never forget. Things started to go downhill almost from the beginning. Clark was late and clearly irritated about meeting with them, Morgan recalls. While Clark read the report from his laptop, he shielded his screen from their view. Prosecutors Becky Holt, Doug Faucette, Deputy District Attorney Howard Cummings, investigator Bill Dowdy, and Morgan looked on in amazement as the doctor sat silently waiting for questions and offering little information. Anyone looking at the scene would not have guessed they were all *supposed* to be on the same side.

Morgan recalls feeling like a game-show contestant searching for the magic question to ask Clark, the one that would make him tell them what they needed to know.

"It was like he wanted to keep everything that he knew, everything that he had done, to himself, and it was almost as if you had to ask him the right question to get the answer to the puzzle," he says. But Morgan adds that Cummings wasn't going to let Clark off the hook that easily. He kept asking the same question in many different ways until Clark finally answered it. He simply wanted to know *what was the exact cause of Eric Miller's death?* The answer was a bombshell—and not what they wanted to hear. Dr. Clark declared that he couldn't be sure anymore if the cause of death was definitely arsenic poisoning. According to Morgan, it was as if the air had suddenly been sucked out of the room, leaving everyone gasping for breath.

Arsenic poisoning was their entire case. Without it, there was no crime. Without it, Ann Miller could never be arrested or convicted. Without it, Eric Miller's murder could never be proven and might remain unsolved forever. The team left the meeting flabbergasted, deflated, and wondering what to do next.

No one spoke until they were out of the building and in the car. Then, Morgan says, all hell broke loose. The usually unflappable prosecutors were pissed off and even talking about ways to charge Clark with some kind of obstruction of justice. They went around and around speculating why the medical examiner would suddenly back down from his original findings at the eleventh hour.

For the first time in a long while, Morgan wanted to get as far away from the Miller investigation as he could.

"I was trying to run for home, a beer, go out and sit in my shed and watch the news, do anything to take my mind off that meeting," he remembers. "This was, I expected, going to be dynamite, a death knell for the entire investigation."

Per Becky Holt's instructions, Morgan had even shown Clark a copy of the Gammon affidavit in which Willard claimed that Ann had confessed to sticking a needle full of poison into Eric's arm. Morgan recalls that Clark was particularly unimpressed by the document. As Morgan saw it, this was a standoff that needed to end peacefully in order to move forward with the case.

Ultimately, Cummings decided that this was a problem for District Attorney Colon Willoughby to fix, and one he would gladly hand over. Cummings asked that every moment of the meeting with Dr. Clark be documented by everyone involved so that Willoughby would know exactly what they were dealing with.

Willoughby set up a meeting with the chief medical examiner of North Carolina, Dr. John Butts. Butts was Clark's boss, an affable man who had never seemed to have issues with prosecutors. After the meeting Willoughby returned to the office and told everyone, including Morgan, that they were going to be able to work it out. Morgan saw this as nothing short of a miracle.

"I have to give him the utmost praise and credit for how he dealt with this situation. Whatever he told Dr. Butts or whatever accommodations he arrived at, it was going to work," Morgan says gleefully. "Dr. Clark eventually was coming around in spite of everything that had happened."

Dr. Clark would stand by his original autopsy report from the spring of 2001, which said that Eric Miller had died of chronic arsenic poisoning; poisoning that had taken place over months, with arsenic that had eaten away at Eric's organs until his body simply couldn't take it anymore. Ultimately, one deadly dose of arsenic was administered on November 30, 2000, resulting in his death. It was the truth, and Dr. Clark was now prepared to assert it in a court of law. Whatever problems Clark had had with prosecutors, at the end of the day he was a doctor and he would tell a jury in his esteemed medical opinion what had *really* happened to Eric Miller.

"It became apparent that Dr. Clark was not going to become an impediment to justice. He was going to stand up and do the right thing," Morgan confirms.

POWER TO THE PEOPLE

In North Carolina, but especially in Wake County, almost all felony cases went to a grand jury for indictment before they landed in criminal court. Even in cases where someone had previously been arrested, prosecutors were reticent to try any felony that had not been validated with a "true bill" (an indictment) from a grand jury. The grand-jury process was one of checks and balances that kept prosecutors from taking faulty cases to court.

There was no doubt that the Miller case was headed to a grand jury first. Ann Miller would not be arrested until a group of North Carolina citizens gave the district attorney's office the green light.

In grand-jury settings, which were always confidential, the defense had no standing. Only the prosecution could offer testimony. Usually this involved just one person, the lead investigator on the case. He or she went into the grand-jury room alone and presented the evidence. The panel was permitted to ask questions. When the witnesses were finished, the grand jury voted about whether or not to indict the suspect. Then they called their next case. The list of true bills was returned to a court clerk at the end of the day. Only then did the information become part of the public record.

Holt and Willoughby decided that Morgan would present the Miller case to the grand jury. While many other investigators had worked hard along the way, no one knew the intricacies of the case like Morgan. By this point Morgan was officially retired and had set up shop in a closet-size space in the district attorney's office. He started crafting a script for the big day. The process was bittersweet, since Morgan knew that even if Ann Miller was indicted, he would not be the one making the arrest.

"I had a recurring dream of exactly how it would go down." Morgan laughs. "Keep Ann looking over her shoulder to see when the fat man in the hat was going to show up."

He had always imagined driving to Wilmington and plucking Ann out of her house, or her office, by surprise. But he knew that as a retired cop with no power of arrest, this wouldn't be the case. Still, he hoped that the grand-jury indictment would be a surprise to her and that whoever ended up arresting her got a chance to catch her woefully off guard.

But alas, there are no secrets in a courthouse. The elevators, the stairwells, the walls themselves seem to ooze information, just waiting for an eager reporter or perceptive lawyer to pick up on.

"Ann Miller knew she was going to be arrested. Her lawyers knew she was going to be arrested. And I think that took a big load of wind out of my sails," Morgan says bitterly.

But he couldn't afford to get sidetracked. Instead, he concentrated his efforts on making the best possible presentation he could to a grand jury. He knew he would have only one chance to do this. If he failed, the case would be over. The standard that had to be met in front of a grand jury to get a true bill returned was probable cause—the same standard needed for an arrest. Clearly, prosecutors Colon Willoughby and Becky Holt felt they had enough to prove the case beyond a reasonable doubt or they would not have taken it this far, but Morgan was still nervous about having the entire future of the case resting on his ample shoulders. It had all come down to this.

With confidence, yet not without emotion, Morgan walked the grand jury through the Raleigh Police Department's case against Ann Miller from the very beginning. He told them about all of Eric Miller's hospitalizations and Dr. Thomas Clark's subsequent findings that arsenic poisoning was the cause of death. He told them about Ann's affairs with Derril Willard and Carl Mackewicz. He told them about his one and only conversation with Willard, about Willard's suicide, and ultimately, about Willard's confession to Rick Gammon regarding Ann putting poison in Eric's IV at Rex Hospital. He walked out feeling like he had done his best.

After Morgan read his notes to the grand jury, he went into the hall and waited. Approximately two minutes later jurors called in the next investigator to testify in the next case. *Bingo,* thought Morgan. They'd had no trouble deciding on a true bill; otherwise the lag time between the two cases would have been longer. He was ecstatic. But there was still the matter of where they could find Ann Miller when the warrant was finally signed and ready to be executed. He had waited too long for this day for her arrest to be a nonevent.

JAILBIRD

Within ten minutes of the signing of the warrant, Joe Cheshire called Becky Holt and told her that his client would turn herself in at the Wake County Public Safety Center. It was to be a civilized handover, not the kind of painful, embarrassing event Morgan had hoped for after all these years. Not only would it be civil, but Morgan would play no role beyond that of an idle spectator on the sidewalk in a big white hat.

He was now, for the first time in his law enforcement career, on the outside looking in. He was no longer part of the show; he was just a civilian on the sidelines gawking like everyone else.

"After all that time it was something of a bitter pill to swallow, but I swallowed it," Morgan says matter-of-factly. "Essentially it was not my rodeo."

Morgan stood across the street and watched as Detectives Amanda Salmon and Justin Matthews placed Ann Miller in handcuffs in front of the jail. In an oversize sweater and tan cotton pants, her shoulder-length now strawberry-blond hair unfixed around her barely made-up face, Ann looked more like a schoolteacher than a cold-blooded killer. She seemed bewildered, as if she couldn't imagine how this could be happening to her, as if a mistake had obviously been made. To Morgan, her demeanor, and even her choice of outfit, was calculated. He figured she wanted to look "mousy" so that people would feel sorry for her.

"She was the prototypical psychopath in sheep's clothing because she truly looked shell-shocked, vulnerable, meek," recalls Morgan. "But I think I was able to see the real Ann as she was. She was just as evil as she'd ever been. She was doing what psychopaths often do. She was acting appropriately for the situation after behaving in a totally inappropriate manner. Ann looked very much the victim that day."

Detectives proceeded to put Ann Miller into a Raleigh police car to take her to the station for questioning. This caused her lawyers to go ballistic, insisting that she had turned herself in and did not need to be processed at the police station.

The only ones who seemed to care that the former investigator in the white fedora was on the sidewalk that day were the media. They surrounded Morgan like hungry barracudas. They pounded him with questions peppered with phrases like "this must be a great day for you," and "you must be happy." While Morgan did experience a flood of emotions that day, happiness wasn't one of them.

" 'What have I got to be happy about? A good man is

dead, two good men are dead. Two children who will never know their fathers as they grow older. There's nothing to be happy about here,'" Morgan says, recalling his words to the media.

The battle was not over. Far from it. It had only just begun. Ann Miller was finally behind bars, but now they had to keep her there.

TEN

*Progress might have been all right once,
but it's gone on too long.*
—OGDEN NASH

In his heart and in his head Chris Morgan fully believed
that Ann Miller (by this time going by her new married
name, Ann Miller Kontz, but Morgan just couldn't bring
himself to call her that) had convinced Derril Willard to
give Eric poison that night at the bowling alley. He also
strongly suspected that Ann had already experimented by
giving Eric small doses throughout the summer of 2000.
And after Eric managed to pull through the first hospitalization, Morgan believed that Ann went back to what was
convenient—more arsenic.

But this theory still was not sitting well with Dr. Marsha
Ford (no relation to Tom Ford), who headed North Car-
olina's Poison Control Division. According to Morgan, Dr.
Ford remained unconvinced that a woman as educated as
Ann Miller would have continued to use such a pedestrian

poison when, as a scientist, she clearly had access to and knowledge of other dangerous chemicals. Especially considering that UNC Hospitals had already determined that arsenic was a factor in Eric's first hospitalization, Dr. Ford felt Ann would not have been stupid enough to use it again.

"She was just wrong about that," Morgan says. "Ann wasn't particularly smart. I mean, they got her school records from Purdue University. I know what she made on the SAT. I scored higher on the SAT than Ann Miller did . . . She wasn't quite a genius. She was a long way from being a genius."

In October of 2004, Morgan and the prosecution team headed to Charlotte to have a meeting with Dr. Ford. Unlike his experience with Dr. Thomas Clark, Morgan recalls that Dr. Ford was pleasant and cordial. He knew she was an eminently qualified toxicologist and that her testimony would be key to putting Ann behind bars. But they didn't want her speculating about other poisons in front of a jury. Morgan was convinced that Dr. Ford, as brilliant as she was, was simply tripping over the fact that an educated scientist would use a generic poison to commit murder. He also felt there was a chance she'd been led down the garden path by the previous prosecutor in the investigation. The only way for Morgan to turn it around was to convince Dr. Ford that her assumption about Ann's intelligence was incorrect.

"Essentially [Dr. Ford] believed that criminals are smart. I mean the legend of the criminal mastermind who outwits the police, outwits prosecutors, outwits medical experts—certainly Ann's occupation would lead you to believe she had that kind of talent," Morgan says. But to Morgan, that was the stuff of made-for-television movies. This was *real life,* and in his experience, real-life criminals are just plain stupid.

"By and large the myth of the criminal mastermind is just that . . . a myth. Most criminals, even psychopaths, are really not that smart. They can be clever, they can be good actors, but they're not grossly overintelligent," Morgan states. "If [Ann] had been a criminal genius, we probably would never have been able to lay a glove on her."

Morgan pleaded his case to Dr. Ford, explaining why he thought Ann Miller was just a typical criminal who happened to have a degree. He explained that she did what a lot of criminals do—she took the path of least resistance. In this case, *arsenic.*

"I staked out my position and I thought I saw something glimmer in Dr. Ford's eye by the time that meeting was over," Morgan says, and sighs with relief. Dr. Ford ultimately agreed with Dr. Clark that Eric had died from arsenic poisoning and that he'd received the fatal dose prior to his final hospital stay.

In a letter to Becky Holt dated April 14, 2005, Dr. Ford said: The fatal cardiac arrest sustained by Eric Miller on December 2, 2000, was the result of the first, and possibly the second dose of arsenic (as described in items 1 and 2 above), and no other etiology or addition toxin need be evoked.

TEAM SCIENCE

In the early days of the investigation Morgan hadn't quite grasped just how important science would be to solving and proving this case. As he did with a lot of things he didn't understand, he had simply shrugged it off. Looking back, he recalls a moment when he'd had just about enough science talk and mouthed off in front of a local newspaper reporter.

"I popped off in the mouth and I said in front of Oren [Dorell], 'People need to remember this is not a science project, this is a murder investigation,' and it pretty much ended up in print," Morgan laments.

Upon reflection, Morgan realized that science *was* the heart of the case. Ann was able to kill Eric because she was a scientist who understood how to use a toxin to end someone's life. So as they prepared for trial, Morgan was finally at peace with the complex science that would be the core of the case.

But it wasn't enough to have just one eminently qualified scientist on their side; Becky Holt told Morgan they would need a team of experts, not just Dr. Clark and Dr. Ford, to win this case.

Holt was looking for someone who knew what they were talking about, someone who could testify in court, someone who would seal Ann's fate.

Early on, they heard that defense attorneys had retained Dr. R. Page Hudson, the former chief medical examiner of North Carolina, who had reigned over the office during the Velma Barfield case, and the Blanche Taylor Moore case, both high-profile arsenic poisonings that captured statewide attention and national headlines. So he was out. This was not good news for the prosecution team, but nonetheless they got to work looking for experts who could support their theory of Eric's death. This was no easy task, since scientists, not unlike investigators and attorneys, don't necessarily share the same opinions even when faced with the exact same set of facts.

Dr. Ken Kulig was a toxicologist in Denver, Colorado, whom investigators interviewed by phone. Almost immediately after reading the clinical records and the test results, he appeared to be on board with what Morgan already knew.

"One of the things that he did confirm for me in our very first conversation was that Eric Miller should, based on his clinical record, . . . have survived the arsenic poisoning that he got on the night of the bowling-alley incident," Morgan says. "You end up dead, or you improve—I mean, there's very little middle ground."

Given the direction that Eric Miller's health took— plummeting twice after he appeared to be getting better— Kulig agreed with Morgan that the theory of multiple poisonings appeared to be correct.

"If anybody could weather the effects of this toxin, it should have been somebody like Eric because he had not only the strength to survive, but obviously, from everything in his clinical records, had an extremely strong will to survive and to overcome this poisoning," says Morgan. "That sort of became a cornerstone of this case. Kulig said emphatically that something happened to Eric once he got home."

In a report to Becky Holt dated April 14, 2005, Dr. Kulig wrote:

> I reviewed the autopsy results very carefully to determine if Mr. Miller died from arsenic poisoning or from something else. The analysis of his clinical course during this time period, his arsenic levels in multiple tissue sites, and the autopsy findings, are unequivocal as to cause of death. I completely agree with the office of the chief medical examiner that the cause of death was arsenic poisoning, and that there were at least two and possibly more instances of arsenic dosing in this case.

In the third scientist, Alphonse Poklis, Morgan found a kindred spirit and possibly the savior of the entire case. He was a big, burly, bearded toxicologist at the Medical College of Virginia who reminded Morgan of Shakespeare's Falstaff, a jovial, gruff man who in one moment was effortlessly gregarious and, in the next, a total curmudgeon. Poklis was also a well-known expert on the topic of arsenic poisoning who probed the investigators as hard as they probed him.

"He may be *the* definitive authority on arsenic poisoning in the world," Morgan states with enthusiasm. "Essentially, poisoning and arsenic is his world. Very few people in the world know as much about it as he does because he has studied it so hard for so long."

Not unlike Kulig, Poklis immediately realized that the plunge that Eric's health took after he was supposed to be getting better could mean only one thing: that Eric had been poisoned *again*.

"[Eric] had taken a long time to get over it, but at his age, and in his [state of] health, he was on the road and he should have stayed on that road had not somebody ambushed him with an avalanche of arsenic that ended up putting him back in the hospital and eventually killing him," Morgan recalls Poklis's take on the case.

In a letter to Becky Holt dated April 16, 2005, Dr. Poklis wrote:

I agree with the autopsy report that Eric Miller, a 30-year-old white male, died as the result of arsenic poisoning. Post-mortem toxicological testing of liver tissue demonstrated that the arsenic concentration was elevated beyond normal values.

Morgan and Holt visited Poklis in Virginia, and at one point he came to North Carolina to pay them a visit. Morgan remembers the day Poklis walked into the grand-jury room at the Wake County Courthouse with vivid clarity. Morgan says Poklis was dressed in a college letterman jacket, a well-worn ski hat, and had a scruffy beard that looked like it was in desperate need of a trim. He recalls District Attorney Colon Willoughby at first thinking he was being tricked, that certainly this husky, disheveled man couldn't be the preeminent scientist Morgan and Holt had been speaking about. But when Polkis started talking, everyone listened. It was clear that he knew his stuff.

"He would have been a very powerful witness for us," Morgan says wistfully.

Would have . . . like many other witnesses in the case, Poklis would never get a chance to tell a jury what he believed.

'TIL DEATH DO US PART

One of the key unanswered questions as investigators and prosecutors prepared for trial was whether this case would be a death-penalty case. In every first-degree murder case the prosecutor must decide if the state will seek the death penalty, or simply ask a jury to sentence the defendant to life in prison. In North Carolina this decision is always made before a case goes to trial in what's called a Rule 24 hearing in front of a Superior Court judge.

In Morgan's estimation, the death-penalty issue was problematic for several reasons. Although he personally believed a poisoning case certainly warranted the death penalty, from previous discussions with Eric's family, Morgan knew that the Millers were very religious and probably not in favor of this type of punishment. He also knew that it might be harder to get a conviction if a jury had to consider putting the only remaining parent of a young child to death. But ultimately, the decision was up to the Wake County district attorney. Colon Willoughby would make the final call, and as long as the judge agreed with the decision, that would be it.

In anticipation of this decision Willoughby asked

Morgan to set up another meeting with the Millers. In November of 2004, Verus and Doris Miller, their two daughters, sons-in-law, and grandchildren, all traveled to Raleigh to participate in the discussion. Morgan didn't purposely keep them in the dark about what Willoughby wanted to discuss, but he didn't go into detail either. He figured no matter what he said, the outcome would be the same.

They met in a conference room one evening at the brand-new Raleigh Police Department District 23 substation. Morgan couldn't help but compare these swank digs with the dingy cubbyholes that he'd worked in for most of his career. But despite the bright new conference room, the topic of discussion was still destined to be dark.

"[Colon Willoughby] was very truthful and up front with the Millers. 'This is probably a death-penalty case, but you have input. I want to know what your thoughts are,'" Morgan paraphrases the district attorney's words.

Morgan says Willoughby explained the options, the death penalty or life in prison, and listed the pros and cons of each. Then he gave the family time to confer among themselves before they gave him their decision. Morgan felt it was exactly the right way to handle this delicate situation. It was in these moments that he understood why some people became cops and others became prosecutors. He admired good prosecutors and increasingly, as Morgan watched Willoughby in action, he decided this D.A. was one of the best.

"They [the Millers] didn't want to take Ann's life

regardless of what she'd done to theirs and to Eric's," Morgan says. "They didn't want to take it, but I'm sure in some ways they did want to see her pay a heavy price."

Morgan had no problem with Ann Miller being sentenced to death, but it wasn't *his* decision. He respected the Millers and their beliefs and knew that Willoughby would do the right thing. In some ways he was disappointed that it wouldn't be a death-penalty case, but the more he thought about it, the more Morgan realized that maybe life in prison would be the ultimate punishment for someone who relished control as much as Ann did.

"I kept thinking, 'What is the greatest punishment for this woman?'" Morgan says. "I've always thought that hell for a psychopath probably isn't death nearly as much as it is sitting in a prison cell."

RULE 24

On November 16, 2004, Ann Miller entered a Wake County Superior Courtroom wearing a navy jail uniform. From what Morgan could see from his second-row seat in the audience, she looked teary-eyed and weary. Once again he felt like she was playing the martyr for everyone, including television news viewers. She waved at the audience, presumably at her family and husband, like a beauty queen in the backseat of a convertible during a small-town parade. Her hand stiffly turned back and forth in an awkward motion as if to say: "You will not break me with your accusations, I am still a winner."

Judge Donald Stephens asked District Attorney Colon Willoughby to proceed with his decision on whether or not he would seek the death penalty.

"Do you believe there's no evidence of any aggravating circumstance or do you simply in your discretion elect to proceed non-capitally?" Judge Stephens asked Willoughby.

"Your Honor, there may be evidence from which there could be an aggravating circumstance, but after reviewing it, I have elected in my discretion to not seek the death penalty upon my review of the evidence and the totality of the circumstances," Willoughby replied.

After the hearing, two things struck Morgan. First, he witnessed Ann Miller, whose fair skin was blotchy and tearstained by this point, mouth the words *I love you* to her husband, Paul Kontz, on her way out of the courtroom. To Morgan it was as if Ann was still in denial that she'd killed one husband, and now she had another one panting at her feet like a puppy dog. Second, as soon as the hearing was over, Nancy Brier, Ann's mother, turned and extended her hand to Verus Miller, Eric's father. He took it politely. The whole exchange lasted maybe two seconds, but to Morgan it was further proof of the Millers' graciousness.

In the hallway, after the hearing, the media crowded around the Millers as Morgan stood in the background like a sentinel protecting the perimeter. He wore his trademark white fedora with a brown feather peeking out of the brim and chewed gum as he stood just behind Verus's left shoulder.

"We feel that Eric did die an agonizing death and we do want justice for our son," said Verus, his voice cracking with emotion as Morgan looked on, his angry eyes peering out just beneath the brim of his white fedora. "But as a family, we just weren't for the death penalty."

"We need to represent our son, there's no one here now to represent him, and we're going to be down here representing Eric. That's what's been for the past four years and it will continue [until] it's all over," Verus went on to say, looking like he was going to break down at any moment. Morgan continued to stand stoically at Verus's side in case he was needed to run interference and help his friend get away quickly. Morgan nodded as Verus talked about the case going in the right direction.

"You don't know where you get the strength from, you just get up in the morning and you have it," said Verus. "I give a lot of credit to our family and friends that are continuing to pray for us."

THE PRICE OF FREEDOM

On December 10, 2004, Ann Miller's attorneys returned to court to ask Judge Stephens to set bond so that Ann Miller could be released from jail pending trial. While most first-degree murder suspects are not offered bond, in North Carolina it is up to the discretion of the judge whether or not to do so in any case.

It was a chilly winter day and Morgan's disposition was also somewhat chilly at the thought of seeing Ann Miller in person again. But he did want to see how jail was affecting her. He hoped not well. Morgan took his place in the row behind the prosecutors' table so that he could get a good clear view of Ann as she entered the courtroom. Naturally he sat with the Millers to lend them support. Respectfully, he took off his white fedora in the courtroom and put it on his lap.

This time Ann wore the standard uniform of the Wake County Jail, a gray-and-white-striped number. But instead of looking woeful and dejected, at the bond hearing she had a bounce in her step and new curl in her hair. Unlike the day of her arrest, when her strawberry-blond hair hung limply around her drawn face, it was now as curly and bouncy as a shampoo advertisement. Ann seemed perky, even bubbly, as she entered the courtroom and took a seat between her attorneys. To Morgan, it was just one more bizarre twist in the life and times of Ann Miller. Even after all of these years he still didn't know what to expect from her.

In the days leading up to the bond hearing, Morgan had sensed that Assistant District Attorney Becky Holt and District Attorney Colon Willoughby were planning something big. He couldn't put his finger on what it was, but he felt strongly that he was being kept in the dark about some very important strategy that was about to unfold.

The detectives who had worked their hearts out for Morgan on the case had sent thousands of pages of case files to the district attorney's office. The D.A.'s investigator, Bill Dowdy, was in turn spending his days copying the files to send them to the defense team as part of the discovery process. Morgan couldn't help but feel a little helpless as he watched the boxes, amounting to four years of hard work, sent off. It was like giving a newborn baby up for

adoption. He almost felt compelled to wrestle the boxes out
of Dowdy's hands and run for the elevator. But it was the
law, and Morgan knew it had to be followed.

"It's a terrible feeling. You do all this hard work, you get
all this information, and then you turn it over to somebody
who's trying to shoot holes in it," Morgan confesses.

The defense testimony at the bond hearing was strong.
Witness after witness testified that Ann had a full life in
Wilmington, North Carolina, with her daughter, Clare, and
new husband, Paul, and her stepdaughter. They told the
judge that Ann was not a flight risk or a danger. They testified that she would never leave her young daughter under
any circumstances, not even to escape prosecution.

"I think that her love for God and Paul and Clare . . .
that she would never hurt them," said Dan Brier from the
witness stand on his daughter's behalf. "She would definitely not be a threat to herself or to anyone in any way
whatsoever."

Her family and friends said they would make sure she
showed up for court. Her new employers at PPD, the pharmaceutical company, said they would allow her to continue
working pending the outcome of the case. To Morgan, things
did not seem to be going well at all. Defense attorneys were
making an admirable case for Ann Miller getting bond.
Something had to turn this train around or Ann was going to
be free again, free after so many years of hard work to get
her off the streets.

"We would like for Ms. Miller to [be] out on bond because it would be good for her," Ann's lawyer Wade Smith
said in his polite deferential tone. "But Mr. Cheshire and I

need her desperately to be on bond because we've got thousands and thousands of pages of material that [we] need her to help us with and that's just the truth, it's just the truth, and I don't know how we do it at the Wake County Jail."

The Wake County Jail was supposed to offer temporary housing for people awaiting trial, but like most county jails in growing cities, it had become almost unbearably overcrowded. The visiting space for attorneys and clients was very limited and rarely available.

Always the southern gentleman, Wade Smith could outpolite just about any lawyer in the courtroom. With his shock of white hair, wire-framed glasses, bow tie, and diminutive stature, he looked more like someone's kindly grandfather than a force to be reckoned with, but in the world of defense attorneys, he was the guy you wanted on your side.

"She has extraordinary close family ties, a remarkable family that will stay in touch with her; they will be together at all times. There's no way that's she's going to hurt herself. There's no way that's she's going to run away. She is absolutely loved by her family and they will look after her," Smith asserted.

Smith called Ann Miller a "church worker" who lived for God and her family. He pointed to the dozens of letters of support in a stack on the table in front of him. It was almost too much for Morgan to take, but even as the disgust welled up inside of him when he heard people talk favorably of Ann Miller, he was still enjoying the show. In his heart he felt sure Judge Stephens wouldn't buy in to the farce that was being played out in his courtroom.

"While we would never use this point, we don't have the child here, we would not do that, we don't make the argument on the child to try to twang Your Honor's heartstrings in some way, the child is important because the child gives her [Ann] life force. There's every reason for this woman to want to live," Smith said forcefully.

"For years she has known this was coming," he continued. "She did not run away. And when it came, the day had arrived, she came to Raleigh to present herself. *Remember* that, Your Honor, she's a marvelous candidate [for bond]."

But just as Morgan had expected, A.D.A. Becky Holt had some fireworks of her own planned for the bond hearing. That nagging feeling that he had had all week that something was in the works was right. Holt wasn't going to let defense attorneys, even the top defense attorneys in the state, outdo her with character witnesses.

Boldly, Holt asked Judge Stephens's permission to read the Gammon affidavit into the record. This was the first time anyone outside of the attorneys, the investigators, and the judge had ever heard the contents of Derril Willard's statement to Rick Gammon. It was more than likely that paragraph 12 would never make it into the trial court as evidence because of the legal hurdles the D.A. would have to cross, but now it would be in an even more influential court in Morgan's mind: the court of public opinion.

Stephens allowed Holt to proceed with the verbatim reading of paragraph 12 while the audience leaned forward and hung on every word. Television cameras zoomed in to make sure they captured the moment in its entirety. Morgan beamed and exchanged hopeful glances with the Millers. Now the information was finally out there for the entire world to know. Even if it were never admitted at trial, it was now public record. Ann's dirty little secret was out. She could deny all she wanted to, but to Morgan, paragraph 12 was the evidence that confirmed her guilt *beyond a reasonable doubt*.

Morgan knew it by heart, but still listened intently to Holt's reading of Ann's evil deed, her admission to Willard that she had taken a syringe and inserted it into Eric's IV while he was a patient at Rex Hospital, and that she'd told Willard the substance was some type of poison.

In Morgan's mind it was irrefutable evidence that would show the world what he had known about Ann Miller all along: she was a cold-blooded killer.

Holt also read Willard's suicide note out loud and into the court record, another document that had been kept under lock and key for four years. In it, Willard denied any responsibility for Eric's death. It was a statement that Morgan now truly believed after learning more about Willard and his relationship with Ann.

"I'm sure Wade Smith and Joe Cheshire were both totally apoplectic. They were in a much bigger state of shock than I was, and I was shocked," Morgan admits.

Judge Stephens said that he had prepared the bond order the night before, but left the terms blank because he wanted to wait and see what transpired at the hearing. He told the court that he had never set bond in a poisoning case before, and needed to take the matter under advisement for a few minutes before he made a decision. He left the courtroom and returned twenty minutes later with his decision.

"I have decided in my discretion to set bond, but I will set a bond appropriate to the nature and circumstances of the charge and the evidence that the state thus far [has shown] as well as the defendant's situation and her local ties and family support," Stephens said, peering over the top of his glasses at the order on the bench in front of him. "I've just signed the order. It reads as follows: 'Upon review of all of the evidence presented, the court in its discretion sets the bond in the amount of three million dollars secured to be approved by the undersigned judge. It's further ordered that the defendant shall reside either in Wake or New Hanover County and shall remain therein unless traveling to court, or to meet with counsel. The court finds that the nature and the circumstances of the alleged offense and of the defendant's situation are such that this bond is necessary to assure the defendant's presence at trial.'"

Morgan exhaled. "It was [a bond] that was impossible for any person who was not a well-connected Colombian drug dealer to make," he says.

In Morgan's mind they had already won the case. Clearly, with a $3 million bond, Ann wasn't going anywhere. And now with paragraph 12 solidly in the court record, he couldn't imagine a jury that would let her off.

"The Millers were looking at me, I was looking at the Millers, my mouth was open, I looked at Becky [Holt], she grinned at me," Morgan says.

LET'S MAKE A DEAL

The case was definitely beginning to take shape, but Morgan had to keep reminding himself that it wasn't a done deal yet.

He personally didn't see anything that was insurmountable, but he also knew that cops and lawyers were different creatures who approached situations in very different ways. What he saw, and what they saw, might be two completely divergent scenarios.

"Lawyers are always concerned, and they're always looking three steps ahead. Cops act on impulse, in large part; even the most seasoned amongst us are typically not great thinkers," says Morgan with a belly laugh.

He knew it was the prosecutors' job to be skeptical, to ask the tough questions, to play the devil's advocate. So like a good soldier, he went along with it for the good of the case. He didn't get his feathers ruffled when Becky Holt and Doug Faucette went over and over points they had already discussed with him a million times. He tried to give them all of the information they needed to build the best possible case against Ann because they had a common goal: putting her away.

They went back to the nuts and bolts of the case, reinterviewing people they hadn't talked to in years. Morgan concentrated on the hospital staff. While they all remembered Eric Miller and his painful death, unfortunately they had little to say about Ann. Morgan had been hoping to find someone who remembered her behaving inappropriately during her husband's hospital stay, or had seen her show some sort of crack in her rock-hard veneer, but while he found glimmers of this, he heard no real evidence that she had given herself away to anyone.

One thing did stick in Morgan's mind, though, after the interviews. Typically, big-time defense attorneys conduct their own parallel investigations in order to be able to refute whatever the state said about their client. They interview the same witnesses. In most cases involving fancy lawyers and deep pockets, the attorney interviews are often conducted long before the police get to these same witnesses. The goal, Morgan imagined, is to take rock-solid witnesses and confuse them, leaving the cops hoping for some tidbit hidden deep down inside their subconscious. But in every interview Morgan conducted in preparation for Ann's trial, when he asked the witnesses if they had been contacted by defense investigators, every time the answer was "no."

"For a while I worried about it. Are we missing something?" Morgan remembers wondering.

The defense team had also not contacted Morgan himself for an interview even though they knew he would be a key witness in the case. This seemed highly unusual to Morgan. Most defense-team investigators were retired cops themselves, who called on officers testifying for the prosecution and tried to pick their brains about the case. But he hadn't gotten a single call.

Finally, in A.D.A. Becky Holt's office, during the early spring of 2005, Morgan simply blurted out the conclusion he had come to.

"I said, 'Becky they're going to try and cut a deal, they're not going to trial,'" Morgan recalls.

Everyone told Morgan he was crazy, that there was no way that after evading arrest for so many years, this woman would roll over so easily. But Morgan was convinced something smelled funny. Top attorneys like Wade Smith and Joe Cheshire left nothing to chance. This wasn't their first rodeo. They knew exactly how to play the game. If they weren't interviewing witnesses, there was a reason, a very good reason.

ELEVEN

Some things have to be believed to be seen.
—RALPH HODGESON

It was time to tie up loose ends. Since they didn't know what the defense team was up to, the prosecution team continued to prepare their case thoroughly. And there was still one very key player who needed to be brought in—forty-four-year-old Carl Eddy Mackewicz, Ann Miller's former lover from California.

Carl Mackewicz had become a focal point early on in the investigation for several reasons. First were the multiple trips to the West Coast that Ann had orchestrated, financed by Glaxo Wellcome in the guise of doing business. But the real motive had been for Ann to see Mackewicz.

During an early search of the Millers' home, Detective Debbie Regentin had spotted a cryptic note in a trash can. It had apparently been written around Valentine's Day 2000, shortly after Clare was born. In the note Ann was trying to explain her relationship with Carl to Eric.

"She essentially said, hey, you know let's kiss and make up. We don't need to let this get blown out of proportion. You know I've got my friends; you've got your friends. We both work in high-contact jobs with the opposite sex. And, don't be concerned, I love only you," paraphrases Morgan.

And then there were the e-mails and phone-call records demonstrating a persistent connection between Ann and Mackewicz spanning years. This included the short story Ann had written that seemed to describe a real romantic interlude that she and Mackewicz had shared in the mountains. Even though it was filled with flowery, fantasy-driven language, Morgan thought he could see it for what it was, reality masquerading as fiction. This fit into Ann Miller's pattern. As far as Morgan was concerned, Ann Miller herself was fiction masquerading as reality.

All of these things had led Jeff Fluck to send a detective to San Francisco in the early phases of the investigation, to drop in on Carl M. Detective Doug Brugger had made the California cold call. Overall, Brugger learned little from the visit, according to Morgan, beyond the fact that Carl Mackewicz was a typical middle-aged California surfer dude who also happened to have a Ph.D.

"He had steadfastly denied any romantic relationship with Ann Miller," Morgan reiterates.

But as more e-mails and phone records started to surface, investigators came to the conclusion that Mackewicz had not told Brugger the truth.

"We reached a point where we realized that Carl had lied to us horribly. I mean, it was obvious that there was history there," Morgan says.

Once the evidence mounted to the point that the affair could no longer be denied, Brugger called Mackewicz, who ultimately confessed that he *had* been having a romantic relationship with Ann for many years.

The couple had first met when Mackewicz, a scientist at the University of California in San Francisco, came to North Carolina to collaborate with Glaxo Wellcome on an antiviral project. At that first meeting on January 17, 1997, he met with a Glaxo biochemist and his then technician, Ann Miller. Mackewicz told police that upon reflection, he barely remembered having met Ann at all. But at some point, after Mackewicz had made multiple trips to North Carolina, Ann started to engage him in flirtatious e-mail exchanges.

On September 2, 1997, Ann e-mailed Mackewicz and thanked him for "beautiful sunsets shared" in San Francisco. He responded by e-mail on September 5 by saying "Guess Who?" and referring to their last meeting as having been like an "awkward" second date. On the same day, about an hour later, Ann responded with "Guess Who Back" and talked about their having spent more than eight hours straight together in their last visit. A week later Mackewicz sent Ann an e-mail letting her know that he was going to be coming to Raleigh the following Monday.

"Carl [Mackewicz] pretty much fessed up: 'Hey, you know maybe there *was* something more between me and Ann than what I told you before. It kind of took me aback when you came out here from North Carolina and I didn't tell you the truth. Here's the real truth. Yeah, we've been

lovers for a couple of years now,' " Morgan says of Mackewicz's confession. Mackewicz had been reticent to come
clean because he had since gotten married and didn't want
his new wife dragged into his past.

The timing of Ann Miller and Carl Mackewicz's last
sexual encounter raised eyebrows among the investigators,
and pointed to another possible motive behind Eric
Miller's murder. In the late spring of 1999, Mackewicz
came to North Carolina again. But this time, instead of
coming for business, Morgan says it seems that Ann and
Mackewicz went to the Outer Banks (a coastal resort), to a
house Ann had rented while Eric was attending a conference in another city.

"We all started counting on our fingers, trying to calcu-
late the possibility that Carl [Mackewicz] could have been
the father, in fact, of Clare Miller," says Morgan.

After more investigation, the math didn't add up; in fact,
it became clear that Ann actually was already pregnant
when she and Mackewicz met for their last romantic weekend. It wasn't a surprise either—Morgan later learned that
Ann and Eric had already begun telling people their good
news prior to that romantic interlude.

"She knows that in her womb she is carrying Eric's
child, but still she is traipsing all over the Outer Banks of
North Carolina and having sex with this individual," says
Morgan with disdain.

But that wasn't what made Morgan home in on Mackewicz as a key player in the case; it was the timing of one
particular e-mail that caught his eye. On Thanksgiving day

in 2000, during Eric's stay at UNC Hospitals, Ann Miller went into her office and sent Mackewicz an e-mail. It was an odd note. She told him that her husband was deathly ill, that her in-laws were driving her crazy, and that she would like to buy Mackewicz a house at the beach and throw a party. At the end of the note she asked him to call her at home during the day, and that her in-laws were oblivious to who called. Morgan thought it was a bizarre message for the supposedly doting wife of a sick husband to write.

Morgan wondered if Carl Mackewicz was the magic bullet—could he be the motive they had been looking for all along?

"Derril Willard was a patsy, he was treated like a patsy [by Ann]," says Morgan. But Ann's relationship with Mackewicz was different. Ann had seemed truly taken with him. No one in the police department had talked to Mackewicz since the summer of 2001. Morgan knew that it was time to have a face-to-face meeting with the man who just might unlock the motive.

FEET ON THE GROUND

Assistant District Attorney Becky Holt agreed with Chris Morgan that it was time to get back in touch with Carl Mackewicz. Her solution was simple—let's fly out to the West Coast and reinterview them. But the proposition wasn't that simple for Morgan.

"I was peculiar about a lot of things, but one of things I

was probably most peculiar about is I don't fly. I have never flown. As far as I know today, I will never fly," Morgan states without apology.

Morgan isn't afraid of dark alleys, mass murderers, or blood-soaked crime scenes, but flying—that is simply not in his repertoire. Dr. Michael Teague even offered to hypnotize Morgan to help him get over his fear, but he would have none of it.

Morgan recalls Holt's firm response to his statement that he wasn't getting on an airplane for anyone. "It wasn't a request, it wasn't a suggestion. She was saying, 'You're going to San Francisco, big boy, we're both going to San Francisco, and we're going on a big silver bird,'" Morgan says with an anxious chuckle.

Morgan's solution to the quandary was to *drive* to California. He told Holt he would get a police car and drive across the country in record time to do the interview. He promised that he would start a few days ahead of her, and even be there in time to pick her up at the airport. Morgan guessed that he could probably find some sucker willing to take the cross-country trip with him so that he wouldn't have to do it alone. But Holt wasn't buying it.

So Morgan came up with an alternative. He suggested that it would be easier for everyone if Mackewicz just came to Raleigh. Morgan recalls that Holt laughed and told him it would never work, that Mackewicz would not *willingly* travel three thousand miles to put himself smack-dab in the middle of a murder case.

"I said, 'Becky, never underestimate the power of a man

who has never been on an airplane to continue his record of not getting on one,'" says Morgan.

REELING HIM IN

Morgan was always up for a challenge, especially when it came to convincing other people to do things and making them think that it was their idea in the first place.

He went down to his cubbyhole-slash-office and got to work. He left an open-ended message on Mackewicz's voice mail saying that he needed to talk with him at length and was planning a trip to California to do so. He added that he was willing to do the interview at Mackewicz's office or his house, whichever location was more convenient for him. Deference was one of Morgan's strengths, when he chose to pull it out and dust it off.

"When you need to get someone to cooperate, the easiest way to do that is to start edging around their home life," says Morgan, recalling how quickly Mackewicz called him back.

When he was involved with Ann, Carl Mackewicz had been happily single, free to dabble. But he was now married, and it was clear to Morgan that he did not want to involve his new wife in this mess. He was also still working as a research scientist at the University of California in San Francisco, which was another part of his life that he desperately wanted to keep separate from his involvement in Eric Miller's case.

In the telephone conversation with Mackewicz, Morgan continued to allude to the trip that he and Holt would be taking to California to meet with him. Morgan's plan was simple. It involved no trickery or masterminding. He just made it clear to Mackewicz that if he and Holt went to the left coast, he wouldn't be able to keep the situation from Mackewicz's family and friends. The more Morgan talked about the potential of having to corroborate Mackewicz's story with other people in his life, namely his coworkers, the more he could feel Mackewicz's anxiety level growing exponentially through the telephone receiver. Morgan could almost picture the poor man leaning back in his swivel chair at his desk, one hand on his forehead, contemplating how what he'd thought was a benign romp in the hay had now landed him in the middle of a nightmare.

When Morgan sensed that Mackewicz was becoming desperate to find an escape hatch, he slowly pitched the idea that Mackewicz might be able to take a few days off from his busy schedule and come east so as to avoid mixing this sticky situation with his personal and professional life. Morgan painted this as a relatively painless option compared to the Raleigh Police Department invading the West Coast with their shiny badges, accusations, and probing questions.

In the end, just as Morgan had anticipated, Mackewicz agreed to make the trip to Raleigh. Morgan thanked him and told him he would be in touch soon with details.

Morgan returned to Holt's office with the good news like a little boy who had just won the spelling bee. He delivered the message in a singsong voice with a sheepish grin and told Holt that Mackewicz would be on their turf in just two weeks, ready and willing to cooperate.

At moments like this, Morgan often wondered out loud if he actually should have been a used-car salesman instead of a cop. Maybe that would be his next career.

WEST MEETS EAST

On February 13, 2005, the day that Morgan was scheduled to pick up Carl Mackewicz at Terminal A of the Raleigh/Durham Airport, he made a sign for him and placed it on the dashboard of his unmarked Crown Vic. The idea was that Mackewicz would be able to spot him when Morgan pulled up to the curb. As it turned out, though, Morgan didn't need the sign. He plucked Mackewicz out of the crowd based simply on Detective Brugger's very accurate description.

"I picked Carl Mackewicz out from fifty yards away with absolutely no problem. He looked very California. Everything about him said: 'Hey, I'm from California and I'm a surfer dude,'" recalls Morgan.

Carl had long black hair, a goatee, and a mustache. He wore slightly tattered jeans, a jean jacket, and a peasant blouse peeking out beneath the jacket. Morgan thought he had a laid-back-cool appearance that didn't give the impression that he tried too hard.

"Even though it was still fairly chilly outside, Mr. Mackewicz arrived in Raleigh, North Carolina, wearing leather sandals," exclaims Morgan, shaking his head as if that was a detail he'd never forget.

THE UNRAVELING

After a pleasant ride from the airport, complete with harmless chitchat, Morgan and Mackewicz went to the Wake County Courthouse to begin the interview a little after ten o'clock that morning. Not unlike peeling the layers of an onion, Morgan needed to unravel the relationship between Mackewicz and Ann Miller layer by layer to see what relevance it might have to Eric Miller's murder.

One point emerged early in the interview. It became crystal clear to Morgan that while Mackewicz may have been a major player in Ann's life, she was simply a bit player in his.

"Obviously Ann was much more infatuated with him than he was with her," says Morgan knowingly. Carl told him that while the sex between them had been fine, okay, nothing spectacular, nothing to write home about, Ann had turned the relationship into something much more substantial than it really was.

On September 25, 1997, at 1:47 p.m., Ann e-mailed Mackewicz and told him she wished she could go to California. "I really miss it—or maybe what I miss is someone?" she wrote, not unlike a coy teenage girl. She also playfully accused him of blowing her off, which he denied in a one-sentence e-mail later that same night. On September 26, at 9:27 a.m., she said in response: "Thank You Oh God, I love your e-mails. Do you have any clue what they do to me?"

"Ann lived a rich fantasy life, she could make up just about any scenario she wanted to, and in some ways for her it became real," Morgan says, explaining his impressions of Ann based on Mackewicz's vision of their affair.

On October 16, 1997, Ann e-mailed Mackewicz and described her day as having been a "thinking a lot about Carl" day. On December 8, 1997, she e-mailed him saying: "I have always been told that I have a very WILD imagination—trust me, you have not even begun to learn what my mind is capable of . . . !!!!"

Morgan found Mackewicz honest and straightforward in his statements. Mackewicz made it clear to him that he was not proud of what he had done, but that he had never honestly sought out a relationship with Ann. He told Morgan that she was the initiator and the aggressor, and that he was simply the foolish follower who figured he had nothing to lose.

The investigator for the Wake County District Attorney's Office, Bill Dowdy, delved further into Ann's fantasy life when he questioned Mackewicz about the short story she had written, "96 Hours." Dowdy is bald, stout, and serious, and Morgan recalls the sight of an old-school, by-the-book cop asking an old hippie about fantasy and sexual innuendo as probably one of the only truly comical times in the entire investigation.

"You have to know him as I do to love him as I do," says Morgan with a Cheshire-cat grin.

But Dowdy persevered and got to the information by doing what he always did, asking thorough questions without reacting in any way to the responses. In Morgan's opinion

Dowdy became a top investigator when he was an officer because he didn't reach for anything or try to insert his own interpretation into the equation. He simply went through the short story line by line and made it clear that fantasy was not something he was ready to accept at face value.

In Ann Miller's "96 Hours," in the entry dated Friday, July 31, 1998, she describes the couple in the story planning their day together in Tahoe. The woman, who speaks in the first person, tells the man that she simply wants to be with him no matter what they are doing. "I enjoyed his company. Why I had come was beginning to become so obvious," Ann wrote. In the entry dated Saturday, August 1, they discuss "trust" and the male protagonist's difficulties in maintaining relationships. "I began to get upset and frustrated," she wrote.

On Sunday, August 2, 1998, as the trip is winding down, the couple experiences tension and the female protagonist becomes "terrified" that the man might be upset with her. "I explained that I wanted nothing more from him as a friend than what he was willing to give," she wrote. "Friendships are so hard for me."

"He [Bill Dowdy] almost got red in the face on several occasions. He just couldn't understand, *what are these people doing?*" Morgan chuckles.

But the tone of the interview turned serious when they talked with Mackewicz about his and Ann's May 1999 trip to the Outer Banks. At this point Morgan learned more about the kind of woman Ann really was than even he already knew.

Even before the trip, there had been little cracks in the

affair; to Morgan it was clear that Mackewicz had been having reservations about what in his mind was supposed to be no more than a casual fling. It had turned into much more than he had bargained for.

On March 31, 1999, at 5:15 p.m., Ann e-mailed Mackewicz and talked about their plans for the relationship. It was clear that she felt like he was trying to end things and she was not happy about this prospect. "[Do you] mean that you have already grown tired of our 'relationship state'—is my 2 years up? Please don't tell me that!" she wrote, going on to say that if he just wanted to be friends, she would grudgingly accept this in order to keep him in her life.

Morgan remembers that when investigators interviewed Mackewicz about the May 1999 Outer Banks trip, he dropped a "small bombshell." Mackewicz told them that he would never have made the trip if Ann hadn't agreed to bankroll *everything* from the plane ticket to the house rental. It simply didn't mean that much to him. Mackewicz left Morgan with the impression that unless it had been free, he wouldn't have been interested.

Morgan knew that around this same time frame, Eric Miller had borrowed money from his father to take care of some bills that had become dangerously past due. From conversations with Eric's parents, Morgan knew that it had been hard for Eric to ask for the money. While Doris and Verus Miller were always willing to help their children, they struck Morgan as people who expected their kids to make their own way in the world. He suspected that money wasn't loaned lightly in a family that believed in hard work and taking financial responsibility seriously. Given this fact, Morgan couldn't believe that Ann had plunked down what probably amounted to several thousand dollars for Mackewicz's plane ticket and the beach-house rental.

Morgan also went over the fact with Mackewicz that Ann had been pregnant during this tempestuous weekend, a fact that Mackewicz emphatically denied knowing at the time. Again, Morgan had a hard time understanding why a woman who had apparently had difficulty getting pregnant would so cavalierly jump into bed with another man during the first trimester of what could have been a difficult pregnancy.

"How could she do this? It was just an example of her character, which I believe is a *psychopathic* character," says Morgan with bravado.

ADIOS FOR NOW

Morgan put Carl Mackewicz on a plane back to California the next day. But he made it clear through e-mails and phone calls that Mackewicz would be subpoenaed to testify at trial. Mackewicz, as Morgan fully expected, was very apprehensive at the mere suggestion of going public with the affair. Morgan knew that once Mackewicz appeared in a Wake County Courtroom, all promises about keeping this sticky situation separate from the rest of his life were off. His name would be in the newspaper and on television for his boss and new wife to see. Yet, at the same time, Morgan felt that Mackewicz was a big boy and should have understood what he was getting himself into.

(Ultimately, Carl Mackewicz's name *was* revealed in open court—by Morgan.)

"Don't do the dance if you can't pay the piper," Morgan quips. "I felt mildly sympathetic for the guy, but I never lost any sleep over the fact of him being terribly embarrassed both professionally and personally by being compelled to explain his torrid affair with Ann Miller in open court."

TWELVE

We do not remember days, we remember moments.
—CESARE PAVESE

Anyone who has ever tried to balance a personal crisis with a stressful job knows it can be a toxic combination. When bad things happen in our lives, the rest of the world doesn't retreat, it just goes on.

Morgan's eighty-year-old mother, Mary-Jo Holder, had been diagnosed with kidney cancer in the summer of 2004, and her health continued to deteriorate while Morgan was pursuing the case against Ann Miller. He juggled his work schedule to accommodate doctors' appointments and chemotherapy. But for Morgan, the crisis was less about the strain it caused in his family, and more about the devastating loss he was already beginning to feel.

"It was one of those terrible times when I had my mother turning to me for advice and for guidance on something in her life. It had always been the other way around.

Through the years I had come to count on my mother as not only my moral compass, but as kind of my oracle," reveals Morgan.

After consulting with many doctors, Mary-Jo, along with advice from her children including Morgan, decided not to have her kidney removed. It would have resulted in many months of hospitalization, ultimately decreasing the quality of what little time she had left. Even in her weakened state Mary-Jo lamented about Morgan spending too much time away from the Eric Miller case to take care of her.

"My mother was a very strong woman. I always felt like she was spending a whole hell of a lot more time worrying about me not getting work done than she was worrying about what was going on in her own body, but it's just the way she was," Morgan says.

Mary-Jo never probed him about any cases because she knew he had to keep things confidential, but she couldn't help but weigh in on the Eric Miller case.

"My mother always used the term *phony* and she said, 'That woman [Ann Miller] is just a big phony, I can tell. She doesn't mean anything she says.' And I think that really irked my mother. My mother always hated for anybody to get away with anything. I mean she never let me get away with things as a child, and she didn't believe people should get away with things, especially bad things," Morgan says with a catch in his throat.

In the spring of 2005, Mary-Jo continued her downward spiral. It was clear to everyone she was entering the last stages of the disease. She required round-the-clock care, and like many independent elderly people, she steadfastly refused to have a nurse. In April of 2005, Morgan boldly moved into Mary-Jo's house to care for her. Because Morgan was *technically* retired (whatever that meant), he would take four or five nights a week and his siblings, who were still working full-time, would split the rest. He was thankful that he was able to be there for her.

April was a blur to Morgan, and then came May, when everything came into sharp focus. Mary-Jo was going to die, it was no longer something in the distant future, and it was going to happen soon. As much as he had emotionally tried to prepare for it, Morgan wasn't ready, not now, not ever. The family called in hospice to help them with Mary-Jo's remaining days.

The night Mary-Jo died, Morgan was spending his first night at home in two weeks. His sister had taken over care of their mother, and when she called Morgan in the middle of the night, he went immediately. Morgan, one of his brothers, his sister, and his oldest son, Daniel, just sat there on his mother's front porch, not saying anything at all. Morgan continually reminded himself that he had known this was coming, but now that it had happened, he had no idea what to do.

"That period of time was one of the more difficult times in my life. It was one of the few times when I felt like I was almost lost," Morgan says solemnly.

FAMILY TIES

On one hand, Morgan had never been more optimistic about the case against Ann Miller. They finally had a trial date—January 2006—things were on track, on go, and Ann was securely behind bars. But between dealing with his mother's death and a new family crisis—his son Gregory had been deployed to Iraq—things in Morgan's personal life had taken a dark turn.

Gregory had graduated from North Carolina State University in the spring of 2004. Following in his father's rather large shoes, he was beginning a career as a Raleigh police officer when his National Guard unit got the call, and he was off. He was no longer a weekend warrior, but a full-fledged soldier in harm's way.

Gregory hadn't complained about his deployment to his father or to the rest of his family. He took it in stride. He was a mechanic in the motor pool stationed at a large air base near Baghdad. Morgan knew that it was not as dangerous as other jobs his son could be doing in Iraq, but this still didn't ease his mind. Gregory didn't tell his father much about what was *really* going on, but Morgan knew secondhand that the base where his son was stationed was subject to mortar fire from the perimeter. It was a thought that kept Morgan awake at night, wondering if the phone would ring, wondering if something bad might happen to Gregory.

"It was a time when I really needed to find something to take the edge off and get away from thinking about that," Morgan recalls.

In June of 2005, Morgan decided that one way to distract himself from the stress he was under was to move to the country, something he and his wife, Kay, had always wanted to do. While they had talked about it many times, for one reason or another their dream had never become a reality.

The small house they'd been living in had served Morgan and Kay well for almost three decades. It was supposed to be a starter home, but somehow life got ahold of Morgan and the starter home had turned into the little castle where his children were born and raised.

"It seems strange that we lived in that little cracker box with four kids living with us," Morgan says jovially.

Unlike many of Morgan's colleagues, Morgan had not slowed down in the eleventh hour of his career. For most people, the final years of their jobs are marked by more money, more responsibility, but overall, less grunt work. Yet this had not been the case for Morgan. In his final years as a cop, he'd found himself running up the down escalator trying to tie everything into a neat bow before he retired. That's one of the reasons why he and Kay had never moved.

Morgan and Kay found a house that felt like it was in the country, but in reality still wasn't too far from the city. Morgan wanted to have neighbors, but he just didn't want to see them on a regular basis. For once in his life he wanted the peace and solitude he had always secretly craved. At first, he worried that the house might be too far out, recalling the days when he was always being called in to work in the middle of the night, but then Kay reminded him that he was technically retired. It was easy for Morgan to forget these days after so many years of running at a breakneck pace. Both Morgan and his wife were enthusiastic about the change and all it represented, a new beginning, a new chapter in their once frantic lives, but it would take some getting used to.

RISKY BUSINESS

In September of 2005, just when things seemed to have quieted down on the Miller case, Morgan got a call from A.D.A. Becky Holt. She told him they needed to have a meeting with the Millers to see if they would consider accepting any kind of plea deal in the case. She told him that the defense had not approached the state about a deal, but it was something D.A. Colon Willoughby felt they needed to consider in the event that the opportunity arose.

"This wasn't something that just happened out of thin air. We had been going at this case and preparing to go to trial. I was told and retold that nobody knew that the defense was going to be interested in any way, shape, form, or fashion in a plea bargain. It was almost a dirty word in a high-profile case such as this," Morgan says.

Morgan was once again given the task of setting up a meeting with the Millers. He called Verus Miller, and after getting up his courage, he worked the possibility of a plea deal into the conversation. Morgan felt bad about dropping this bomb over the phone. He had always been one hundred percent honest with Verus, but at this moment he felt like he was letting him down. Still, Verus's reaction surprised him. Verus wasn't shocked at all. It was almost as if he had expected all along that it might come down to *this*.

As a result of the conversation, the entire Miller clan once again traveled to Raleigh and met with the prosecution team on a Saturday morning in early fall. Verus and Doris Miller were accompanied by Pam, Leeann, and their respective spouses. They toured the courthouse, visited the courtroom where the trial was expected to be held, and learned more about the process. But this was just the pregame show. The real reason for the visit was about to take place in the grand-jury room, a big open space bathed in the traditional North Carolina Indian-summer sunlight.

Morgan remembers that the district attorney wasted no time in getting to the point. Willoughby told the Millers that he was still preparing to go to trial, but that the question might arise as to whether or not a plea bargain could or would be struck. He said he had not yet been approached by the defense team, but expected that it might happen.

Morgan recalls both Doris Miller and her daughter Leeann becoming very emotional at the mere mention of a plea bargain.

"I mean there were a couple of, well, there were tearful outbursts from both Doris Miller and from Leeann where they, you know, they emphasized they didn't believe it would be right to come all this way and end up cutting any kind of a deal with Ann, and their outrage was pretty clear," Morgan says.

Assistant District Attorney Doug Faucette took control of the meeting by going around the table and polling each person on his or her views regarding this issue. It appeared to Morgan that Faucette was genuinely interested in finding out what everyone thought about the subject, from the Millers to each member of the prosecution team.

Morgan considered the question very carefully. His concern about going to trial had to do with the strange power that Ann Miller seemed to have over people, especially over men. Morgan pictured her demurely dressed in a high-collared blouse, speaking just above a whisper from the witness box, in front of a jury. This image alone put a flashing neon "Reasonable Doubt" sign in his head. Throughout his many years on the investigation Morgan had interviewed dozens of people—men, women, neighbors, fellow churchgoers—who had been taken in by Ann's charming ways. A number of women had staunchly defended Ann, telling Morgan that he was "barking up the wrong tree" if he even considered that she had something to do with Eric's death.

"I said, 'Could a jury of twelve people, a majority or probably a good percentage of them being men . . . could she cast her spell on them from a courtroom, from the defendant's chair in a courtroom?' " Morgan worried.

People had adamantly supported Ann Miller to the point that Morgan was sure she had an almost mesmerizing power to convert people to her way of thinking. It was a power that had worried Morgan before Ann was arrested, and now it was a power that frightened him when he considered putting her in front of a jury of her peers.

"Juries [often] ignore the facts and focus on the defendant's personality, and with Ann Miller's personality that really scared me, because really, all it would take would be one juror to be taken in by her ability to appear [as] something drastically different [from] what she was," Morgan remembers telling Willoughby that day.

Morgan felt confident that if there was a hung jury in the trial, Willoughby would opt to try Ann Miller again. But he knew that they would never go for a third go-around if the jury hung twice. Morgan also felt strongly that after all they had been through, the Millers could not emotionally handle multiple trials. He also knew that if the jury hung, and Ann got out of jail pending another trial, she would again have access to her daughter, Clare. This was something Eric's family had tried to avoid at all costs. They wanted Ann to have nothing to do with Clare as long as they had a say in the matter.

Morgan sat back and took stock in what he had invested in the case. It was like standing in line for a ride at a crowded amusement park; if you get out of line before the ride begins, all the waiting has been for nothing. Morgan wasn't about to get out of line, even if it meant forgoing a trial in favor of a sure thing, a plea deal that would send Ann to prison for a long, long time. He also reminded himself once again that while he adored the Millers, he did not work for them; he worked for one person in every case. The victim. In his heart he felt that going for the sure thing, the plea deal, would be in the best interest of "his client," Eric Miller.

As they went around the table Doris Miller and Leeann emotionally reiterated their strong concerns about a plea deal. But when it came time for Verus Miller to voice his opinion, Morgan recalls the tone of the discussion changed. In Morgan's mind, Verus truly understood Ann's potential to deceive, and just how dangerous that trait might be on a witness stand. Verus restated Morgan's point of view in more powerful terms. He, too, thought going to trial was risky business.

Morgan says Verus's priority, like his, was keeping Clare out of Ann's hands as long as possible—since the arrest, Clare had been staying with Ann's sister, Danielle Wilson, and her family in Wilmington, North Carolina—and that a plea deal was a good and definite way to achieve this goal. Clearly, Verus Miller wasn't happy about this turn of events, but he could live with it.

Morgan said Pam echoed her father's sentiments, as did Doug Faucette, and investigator Bill Dowdy. Morgan said Becky Holt, on the other hand, looked like someone had punched her in the stomach. He knew that she had put a lot of work into the case and had expected it to go to trial. Morgan understood her anguish personally.

Willoughby thanked everyone for their input and said he would work on a possible offer in the event the defense approached him about a deal. The range he said would be somewhere between twenty-five and thirty-five years on a second-degree murder charge and conspiracy to commit murder. The best part of the whole thing in Morgan's mind was that if Ann decided to take the plea offer, she would have to stand up in open court and admit that she had killed her husband. It was something Morgan had waited for for almost five years.

CLOSURE FOR STEPHANIE

Very little stayed the same in Morgan's life, but every October there was one constant, the North Carolina State Fair. From corn dogs, to upside-down rides, to corny games on the midway, Morgan loved it all—the smells, the sounds, the people, and of course, the extra cash. For years Morgan had worked as a security officer during the weeklong event. Eventually, he had graduated into a position of managing the security detail of off-duty police officers.

It was late October 2005. Unlike past years Morgan was not worried about what he was missing at the police station, or whether he would be pulled from his moonlighting job to attend to more pressing needs at work. He wasn't a police officer anymore. It was a new day. Morgan was free to wallow in the smells of onion rings mingling with the screams from the Tilt-A-Whirl. But even in the middle of this redneck paradise, he still couldn't let the Miller case go. He knew that the case would now most likely end with a plea deal, a decision he second-guessed daily.

"I think that riding around in late October under the blue beautiful North Carolina sky, it all started to come down on me in a way. It was a time, you know, when I had a lot of doubts. Had we done the right thing?" Morgan says.

It was at this moment, under the same clear blue sky at the North Carolina State Fairgrounds, Morgan learned that another chapter in his cold-case file was nearing closure. He got a call from a police friend who told him that an arrest had been made in the Stephanie Bennett murder.

It was something he had never expected, yet always hoped for.

Detective Ken Copeland had been assigned to the Bennett case when Morgan left. Copeland had been working security at the state fair that week, but had been a no-show on several shifts because, he told Morgan, he had to deal with some issues at work. This was not uncommon for officers, and it hadn't raised a red flag with Morgan, until now.

The arrest was a bittersweet victory for Morgan. On the one hand, he had failed to solve the case despite what he thought was his best effort. On the other, he cared deeply for Stephanie's family, and as with the Millers, he had become hopelessly entwined and invested in achieving justice for them in this case. The bitter part was really that no one had kept him in the loop despite the more than two years that he had worked on the case. Like a common civilian, he learned most of the details of the arrest from the television news.

Ultimately, Drew Planten, a chemist with the North Carolina Department of Agriculture, had been linked to Stephanie's murder through DNA. There was already talk that Planten might be a serial killer who had left victims in other parts of the country.

Reporters called to congratulate Morgan. This was uncomfortable because he had to make it clear that he had played no part in solving the case. Instead, he gave the detectives, Ken Copeland and Jackie Taylor, their proper due, saying they had picked up the ball and run with it where he, Morgan, had left off. They solved the case, not him.

Carmon Bennett also called Morgan and thanked him

for everything he had done. Morgan reiterated that he had nothing to do with solving the case, but Carmon's thanks were less about the arrest and more about the shoulder Morgan had offered to a grieving father over the years.

Copeland called Morgan to say that he was sorry for not keeping him in the loop, but that he had been told to keep everything close to the vest because of the sensitive and high-profile nature of the case. He thanked Morgan for allowing him to work on the case. Morgan, in turn, said he wished Ken had been on the case from the beginning, because if he had, it might have been solved years earlier.

At the end of all of the conversations it was still just Morgan alone with his tortured soul, tooling around the North Carolina State Fairgrounds on a golf cart under a perfect blue sky. For the first time in a long while he had a feeling of contentment, a feeling that all the arduous steps he had taken in his career had finally led to this day. Maybe things hadn't turned out exactly the way he had planned, but either way there would be justice for Stephanie Bennett and Eric Miller.

THE FINAL CHAPTER

When Becky Holt called a few days later to say that Ann Miller would take the plea and spend a minimum of twenty-five years in prison, it was anticlimactic. Morgan had known from the day he met with the prosecution team in the grand-jury room that Ann Miller would never go to trial. It was a conclusion he had made peace with. Holt told him Ann would formally enter her plea and be sentenced at a hearing in November.

At the same time Morgan learned that his son, Gregory, would be returning from Iraq. It was almost as if the stars were aligning for the first time in his crazy life. His boy was coming home and Ann Miller was going away.

Holt and Willoughby asked Morgan to prepare a summary of the case to read in open court at Ann's sentencing. Unlike his grand-jury testimony, Morgan knew this speech would not change the outcome of anything that happened in the courtroom. It was merely an opportunity for him to look Ann straight in the eye and tell her he knew *exactly* what she'd done and how she'd done it. He had known for years, and now the world was going to know as well.

"I remember walking into court that morning certainly with mixed emotions," Morgan says, still wishing in some ways that the journey to that day had ended in a trial instead of a plea.

As always, it was Ann's appearance that got to Morgan. Her hair was longer this time, straight and shiny, full of blond highlights. When she leaned forward, it obscured her delicate features. She was dressed like a stylish librarian in a black sweater that hugged her petite frame and a wool pleated schoolgirl skirt. As she entered the courtroom she looked down at her feet bashfully, more like a woman on her way to the gallows than on her way to make a deal. But at one point she turned back to look over her shoulder at her family with a sheepish and inappropriate grin, and that's when Morgan saw the real Ann Miller. For a moment he'd almost been taken in by her demure appearance. *Almost.*

"She didn't look like she could hurt a flea, let alone poison her husband to death with arsenic," says Morgan.

"Mrs. Kontz, did you and Derril Willard conspire to commit the first-degree murder of Eric Miller by means of poison?" Judge Stephens asked Ann, who was now standing in between her attorneys, Wade Smith and Joe Cheshire, at the defense table in front of the bench.

"Yes, sir," she said barely above a whisper.

"Ma'am?" he asked again, as if reading Morgan's mind. Morgan wanted to make sure everyone in the courtroom heard her answer.

"Yes, sir," she said a little bit louder.

"Mrs. Kontz, did you with malice, unlawfully, and intentionally participate in causing the death of Eric Miller?" asked the judge.

"Yes, sir," Ann said.

And then it was Morgan's turn to get on the stand and read the findings-of-fact that he had prepared for this day. In his crisp white shirt and smart yellow tie, he felt like he was on top of the world, but his real feeling of power came when he looked over at Ann and realized she was looking down. She couldn't listen to what he was saying. Morgan assumed it was shame, not guilt, that made his presentation so uncomfortable for her to hear.

The following is the script that Morgan read from in open court that day:

At 2:50 AM, December 2, 2000, Dr. Eric Dewayne Miller died at Rex Hospital in Raleigh. Dr. Miller had been taken to Rex Hospital in the early morning hours of December 1, 2000, for severe gastro-intestinal symptoms, (nausea, vomiting, and diarrhea). In the late afternoon of December 1, 2000, doctors treating Dr. Miller were informed of test results, from an earlier hospitalization at UNC Medical Center, which clearly indicated that Dr. Eric Miller was a victim of arsenic poisoning. Officials at Rex Hospital subsequently notified the Raleigh Police Department and Officer Ford was sent to the hospital. At the time of Dr. Miller's death a homicide investigation was begun by the Raleigh Police Department.

Eric Dewayne Miller was a 30-year-old post doctoral research scientist employed at the Lineberger Cancer Research Center at UNC Hospitals. Eric was married to Ann Brier Miller, also 30 years old, and employed as a research scientist at the former Glaxo Wellcome Company (now GlaxoSmithKline) at Research Triangle Park. The Millers had been married in 1993. They met while they were both students at Purdue University. They had one child, Clare, born in January of 2000. They were residing in a single family residence at 804 Shady Maple Lane in Raleigh.

On November 16, 2000, Eric Miller went to the Rex Hospital emergency room, suffering from extreme nausea, cramping in the abdominal region, vomiting and diarrhea. The onset of his symptoms began after a bowling outing with three of his wife Ann's co-workers at the AMF Bowling Center on Delta Lake Drive in Raleigh. He had gone home and his symptoms continued to worsen to a point where his wife accompanied him to the hospital in the early morning hours of November 16.

During his hospitalization the cause of his symptoms remained a mystery to the doctors attending him. It was suspected that he had some sort of viral infection, but this could never be confirmed. His symptoms continued to worsen and he was transferred to UNC Hospitals from Rex after several days. Shortly before his transfer to UNC Hospitals, a heavy metals test was run on his blood, as one of the doctors treating him thought his symptoms might be as a result of exposure to arsenic. This testing was done at an out-of-state lab and the results were not communicated to the Rex lab until after Dr. Miller had been transferred to UNC Hospitals. The doctors at Rex did contact UNC Hospitals with the results, but a miscommunication resulted in the arsenic levels being understood to be urine levels, rather than blood levels. The reported levels in a urine specimen would not have been a cause for great concern. While at UNC Hospitals, Eric gradually began to improve. On November 24, 2000, he was discharged from UNC Hospitals and sent home to recuperate. Prior to his discharge, a urine sample was obtained from Dr. Miller and sent to an out of state laboratory for heavy metals analysis.

In the following week Eric showed slow but steady signs of improvement according to his parents and doctors. Dr. Drossman at UNC Hospitals, who saw Eric Miller on the morning of November 29, 2000, described his condition as "much improved" from what he had observed of Eric's condition during his hospitalization. Dr. Furman, Eric's family physician, saw Eric on the morning of November 30, 2000, for a follow-up appointment, at which time Eric reported he was feeling better and his appetite was improving. Dr. Furman noted that Eric had no complaints of gastro-intestinal symptoms at the time of this examination. By the afternoon of Thursday, November 30, he felt well enough to go out for a short walk around the cul-de-sac in front of his house with his father; this was his first walk outside in over two weeks. That evening at approximately 5:45 PM, Eric's parents, who had been helping care for him, went out for dinner, leaving Eric at home with his wife Ann and their infant daughter Clare. Ann Miller later reported, in her only statement to Raleigh Police detectives, that she and Eric ate together that night and had a chicken and rice dish that some friends from their church had brought over. Eric's parents returned to the home at approximately 7:15 that evening.

Later that night, at about 11:00 PM, Eric began having terrible cramps, nausea, diarrhea and vomiting. He was again taken to the Rex Hospital emergency room around 4:00 A.M. on Friday, December 1, 2000. His condition continued to worsen during the day and into the evening. During the afternoon, doctors at Rex treating Eric were contacted by doctors at UNC Hospitals and informed that the results of testing done on the urine sample taken from Eric on his discharge from UNC Hospitals on November 24, 2000, had been received. The lab results showed Eric had extremely high levels of arsenic in his system at the time the sample was obtained.

Doctors at Rex Hospital subsequently called the police and a very brief statement was taken from Eric, who was in a very poor physical condition. He was asked if he knew anyone who might be responsible for poisoning him, or if he had taken poison himself. He told the officer who interviewed him that he had not taken any poison and did not know of anyone who might have given him poison.

Eric Miller's condition continued to decline during the night of December 1, 2000. He was placed in intensive care and at 2:50 AM on December 2, he died. An autopsy was performed at the Office of the Chief Medical Examiner, which determined that the cause of death was arsenic poisoning.

Investigators began to investigate the circumstances of Eric's death. On the evening of December 2, 2000, Ann Miller was interviewed at the Raleigh Police Department. During that interview she was asked if she knew of anyone with any motive to harm her husband, she mentioned that Eric had been involved in a minor dispute with a neighbor involving several other residents of their neighborhood over a fence; she could not provide any other possible reason for someone wanting to harm Eric. After that interview, despite numerous attempts to ask Ann Miller additional questions, she refused, through her father and then her attorney to answer any questions from the police department.

On December 2, while at her parents' house, Ann

Miller announced her intention to have Eric's remains cremated to Verus Miller, Eric's father. She subsequently reiterated her intention to go through with the cremation at a meeting to discuss the funeral arrangements at St. Francis' Church on the following day. On both occasions, Eric's parents and sisters were shocked and objected, as the family had no experience with cremation in the past and the subject had never been a topic of discussion by Eric. Eric's father actually offered to pay for all the expenses of a traditional funeral in lieu of cremation, but Ann Miller would not relent

Eric Miller's life was closely examined and it was found that he was very popular and well-thought of by his friends, neighbors, and co-workers at UNC. No one could provide any motive for someone to harm him. There was an extensive search conducted of the lab he worked in and no arsenic or arsenic-containing compounds were located. His e-mail, phone records, and office were searched and nothing suspicious was located. No evidence of any substantial conflict could be found in his life.

During the investigation it was determined that Ann Miller did have access to arsenic in the lab she worked in at Glaxo Wellcome. Several arsenic containing compounds were used by her and her co-workers, and there was no system to track how these arsenic-containing compounds were dispensed.

Ann Miller's cellular telephone records were obtained through court order and it was discovered that there were a large number of calls to one of her co-workers, Derril Willard. Some of the telephone calls placed by Ann Miller to Derril Willard were late in the evening or very early morning hours and the phone records indicate that some of the calls were over thirty minutes in duration. These phone calls began on October 30, 2000, and ended on December 2, 2000.

Derril Willard had been one of the three male co-workers of Ann Miller who accompanied Eric Miller on the bowling outing on November 15. The other co-workers, who had gone bowling with Eric, Randy Bledsoe and Tom Conselor, were interviewed. They both recalled that Eric had consumed part of a cup of beer that had been purchased and poured by Derril Willard, about an hour before he became ill. At the time he drank the beer Eric made a comment to the other men that the beer tasted "funny or bad." Prior to consuming the entire cup of beer, Eric accidentally spilled it, according to Randy Bledsoe. Within two hours, while bowling, Eric Miller became very ill. He continued to bowl, but was so nauseated he kept a trash bag nearby to vomit in.

Due to the large number of telephone calls between Ann Miller and Derril Willard, investigators attempted on numerous occasions to contact Willard during mid-December 2000. Mr. Willard did not return any messages left for him. Subsequent searches of Ann Miller's work computer revealed numerous e-mails between her and Mr. Willard. These e-mails were of a flirtatious, intimate nature and were indicative of a romantic relationship between the two. It was discovered, however, in analyzing both the telephone records and e-mails that they started in mid-October of 2000, and ended, abruptly, after the death of Eric Miller.

As investigators looked further into the activities of Ann Miller and Derril Willard, it was discovered that they had both traveled to Chicago, Illinois, on November 11, 2000. Ann Miller had told Eric she had to travel to Chicago on business for Glaxo Wellcome; this was reported to Eric's parents who he talked with by phone frequently. A check with officials at Glaxo Wellcome revealed that neither Ann Miller, nor Derril Willard, made the trip to Chicago for a business purpose. They [the company] had no records showing them being sent there or asking for reimbursement for the trip. A check of airline records showed roundtrip tickets purchased on Flight 1300 to Chicago on Southwest Airlines for November 10, 2000, and returning November 12, 2000, in the names of Ann Miller and Derril Willard. The tickets had been purchased at the same time and paid for in cash. A short time after their flight arrived in Chicago, Derril Willard checked into a room at the Chicago Ritz-Carlton, he signed the registration for the hotel room, listing Mr. and Mrs. Derril Willard as the occupants of the room.

Subsequent interviews with Mrs. Yvette Willard revealed that she had not gone to Chicago the weekend of November 10, 2000. She had been in Raleigh that weekend. She did remember her husband making the trip. He had told her he was going to reunite with some friends from college for a weekend outing.

Ann Miller and Derril Willard flew back to Raleigh from Chicago on Sunday, November 12, 2000. A check of the records for the room rented at the Ritz-Carlton showed a room service bill for several in-room meals. This trip was the weekend prior to the bowling outing where Eric Miller was first poisoned.

Among the e-mails and other documents recovered in a search of Ann Miller's work computer were a large number of e-mails and other documents relating to her relationship with a Mr. Carl Mackewicz, who is a research scientist with the University of California in San Francisco. These e-mails and documents dated back to 1997. The content of them plainly showed the existence of an intimate, romantic relationship between Ann Miller and Mr. Mackewicz stretching from mid-1997 until the time of Eric Miller's death. Investigators were sent to San Francisco, California, to interview Mr. Carl Mackewicz. He initially denied any romantic relationship between them, but when confronted with the e-mails recovered from Ann Miller's computer he admitted they had been involved in an extramarital affair for some time. At the time Mr. Mackewicz was divorced. He admitted that they had sexual relations on several occasions when Ann Miller traveled to the west coast for job-related seminars and other reasons. Mr. Mackewicz told investigators that he had traveled to New York City in December 1998 for a rendezvous with Ann Miller, where they spent several days together in a hotel, sightseeing and attending Broadway shows. He also stated that he had traveled to North Carolina and had spent several days at the Outer Banks with Ann Miller in May of 1999. He stated that this was the last physical encounter where the two had been intimate, but they had remained in contact with each other by e-mail and telephone. Mackewicz was questioned about the cost of these trips and informed detectives that Ann Miller had paid for them, including his airfare from California and all lodging expenses. He emphasized that had Ann Miller not paid for these trips he would never have gone on any of them. Mr. Mackewicz stated that he had last spoken to Ann Miller on Thanksgiving Day, 2000. He called her in response to an e-mail she sent him requesting that he call.

Dr. Thomas Clark of the Office of the Chief Medical Examiner performed an autopsy on Eric Miller. His report clearly indicates that Eric Miller received multiple doses of arsenic during the summer of 2000, based on the analysis of hair samples taken from Eric Miller. These doses started as early as mid-June of 2000, and continued into the fall of 2000. The amount of arsenic ingested, based on the hair analysis and clinical record, suggests that the doses during the summer of 2000 were small and not sufficient to induce acute symptoms. Dr. Clark addresses the proximate cause of Eric Miller's death in his autopsy report, saying: "Death is due to arsenic poisoning, with the first dose being prior to the first hospitalization. Laboratory findings are most consistent with the administration of at least one additional dose of arsenic during the prolonged hospitalization. It is possible, based on the clinical history, and supported laboratory studies, that a third dose was administered as well, leading to the final hospitalization." In addition to Dr. Clark, several other experts have consulted on this case. With some variations, these experts substantively agree with the findings of Dr. Clark as outlined above.

It has been clearly established through this investigation that Derril Willard was not in contact with Eric Miller at any time after the night of November 15, when the initial poisoning occurred. During the solitary interview with Ann Miller she never mentions having any visitors during the time Eric's parents went to dinner on the night of November 30, 2000. She never mentions at any time during that interview, or in any conversations with her family or Eric's family, before or immediately after his death, the name of Derril Willard.

Derril Willard was spoken to only once by officers. On January 21, 2001, a search warrant was executed for his residence. I had a brief conversation with Mr. Willard. At that time I told him I felt he was being used by a woman. Derril Willard responded: "Yes, and she is doing a good job of it." He then asked if he could call his lawyer and no further conversation of a substantive nature ensued. The next day, January 22, 2001, Derril Willard was found dead from a self-inflicted gunshot in the garage of his residence. Willard left a suicide note, which was found near his body. In the note he states that he is "not responsible for the death of any-one" other than himself.

When Morgan's song and dance was over, it was Ann's turn. At sentencing, defendants have an opportunity to speak to the judge and the court, to express remorse about their actions and apologize if they so choose. In many instances defendants are too anxious to speak and instead ask their attorneys do it for them. Ann Miller opted to have Joe Cheshire read her statement.

"For reasons I do not now understand I permitted myself to knowingly participate with Derril Willard in events which cost my husband his life. I feel a deep sense of remorse and regret that things happened," Joe Cheshire intoned, reading the words he told the court Ann Miller wrote.

"I will struggle for the rest of my life for how this could have happened. Most of all I regret it for my husband Eric and his family. I also regret it for my husband, daughter and for my family. They are all good and decent people," Cheshire went on as Ann sobbed at the table next to him, "and do not deserve the pain they have suffered. I have asked God to forgive me and I hope that God will also help those others who I have hurt to find it in their hearts one day to forgive me as well. No punishment I will receive today can compare to the pain and remorse I feel in my heart that I was a knowing instrumentality in the death of my husband. I will never get over this event, but I will try to answer my duty to God's law and man's law with humility. In doing so I hope and pray to be able to move ahead and one day to receive forgiveness in this world and the next. Signed Ann Miller Kontz."

And then it was Eric's turn. While he couldn't speak for himself, his family spoke for him, eloquently, graciously, and with the weight of grief hanging over every word.

"Eric was a kind and loving and considerate young man. He was a wonderful son, and brother, and a wonderful father to his daughter in the short time that he spent with her," said Doris Miller as she stood stoically at the end of the prosecution table looking up from her notes periodically to catch the judge's eye.

"I can see him as a child, running through the house, laughing and playing with his *Star Wars* figures, his Matchbox cars. I can look out the window and see him riding his horse in the corral. I drive by the school and I see him playing tennis on the courts," Doris Miller said, pausing as if she were sifting through these past images in her mind.

"He was so happy when he graduated from high school. He went off to college. He was going to accomplish so much. He wanted to help mankind. He graduated from Purdue and came down here and I remember he discussed the accomplishments he made when he got his doctorate in biochemistry. He was so happy with what he was doing with his research in pediatric AIDS. He wanted to make a difference. He wanted to help children. He wanted to help people, but I most of all remember his wonderful smile, and the gleam in his eye when he held his infant daughter. He was such a proud father and he loved her so much. And one day he said to me, he said Mom you always said you loved me, he says now I understand exactly how much." Her voice heavy with pain, Doris Miller bowed her head for about thirty seconds and then continued.

"Ann, you murdered my son," she said, looking across the courtroom at her former daughter-in-law. "He died a cruel and agonizing death that no one should ever have to suffer, especially someone who loved you so much. You can never, ever, spend enough time in prison, enough years. I have a hole in my heart and pain in my chest every day and with every breath I take. You have taken my son from me. I won't ever hold him again. He will never sit at my table. I will never see his smile. You have taken him physically away from me but you can never, ever take his love for us, and you can't ever take away our love for him, and most of all you can never, ever take away my precious memories."

Doris walked back to her seat in the front of the courtroom and embraced her daughter Leeann before sitting down. Morgan only wished there was something he could do to alleviate some of the grief from this broken family. While he knew that making these statements was cathartic for them, he also knew it was emotionally draining in a way that even he could never truly understand.

Verus Miller took his place at the end of the prosecution table with a pile of photographs in front of him. He sat in a chair and shuffled through the pictures, describing each one to the judge. Eric at Christmas, Eric playing tennis, Eric with his sisters, Eric on his horse, Eric with his daughter. With each photograph his voice became more and more agitated until finally, he was almost yelling.

"I wonder what Ann's favorite picture is of Eric? I've got an image in my mind that I'm going to share with you, an image of Eric lying in a hospital bed dead with a tube sticking out of his mouth where the doctors had tried to resuscitate him. I have a picture of him lying in the casket. He didn't look like himself. I have an image of him being cremated—that killed my wife, that killed Doris. I couldn't see why that had to happen. Now I see why it had to happen. I can't understand this, so I'm going to call it evil, and I don't say that lightly," said Verus, looking right at Ann, whose head was bowed, her face obscured by her shiny blond mane.

"In her statement she says 'I don't know why I did this,' or something to that effect. She wants forgiveness? Where's the forgiveness been for the last five years? Yeah, she's sorry, she's sorry she got caught," Verus said, his upper lip and white mustache trembling. "I didn't hear those words out of her mouth, I heard them out of her attorney's mouth. Can't accept them as sincere when they don't come out of the person it's supposed to be coming out of. Just lacks sincerity. Wouldn't surprise me a bit if they weren't written by her attorney."

Verus Miller asked the judge for a moment and then continued. "It haunts me to know that Eric will never enjoy the things that I've enjoyed in life because it was cut short by evil. And you can see evil in this world every day. Just watch your television and read the newspaper. It haunts me that he will not be able to see Clare grow up and graduate and accomplish things that I was fortunate enough to see with my children. And he's dead, Ann, and you're alive, and your parents will still be able to see you, but we'll never see Eric again."

Pam Baltzell, Eric's sister, stood up to read her statement and directed every word at Ann. She punctuated her sentences with wild hand gestures and, at one point, had to quell her emotions when the judge peered at her with concern over the rim of his glasses.

"Why, Ann? Why did you brutally murder my brother Eric?" Pam shouted. "Poisoning him, watching him suffer? Why? I've racked my brain trying to make sense of this, but the only explanation I can find is the fact that there is pure evil in this world. Evil comes in all types of packages. Today we are looking at pure evil. The only thing that Ann Brier Miller Kontz is sorry about is the fact that she was caught."

And then it was Leeann's turn to speak. She also stood and directed her comments at Ann. But unlike Pam's words, which were at a fever pitch right out of the gate, Leeann's anger grew throughout her statement, and eventually boiled over at the end.

"There's no way to quantify how his absence has and will affect us all," said Leeann, wiping away a constant flow of tears. "But Clare, his daughter, has definitely lost the most. She will have no memories of her father and will not benefit from his complete love and devotion to her and attention to the moral and spiritual guidance he would have given. I don't believe that you, Ann, truly love your daughter. How could you when you have taken away one of the most precious gifts that she will ever have—her father? Why would you set her up to face a life of difficulty and trauma as she grows and begins to understand that her mother poisoned and killed her father and betrayed him in multiple other ways with affairs and lies?" Leeann said directly to Ann, who was hunched over the table as Joe Cheshire tried to block her from the television cameras' view.

"A child is the ultimate and most precious gift from God and you do not deserve to be her mother. I find tremendous comfort in knowing that you will be removed from Clare's life, thus protecting her from further pain or danger inflicted by you. I will continue to pray for her to be strong and to overcome the hurdles that you have placed before her," Leeann said.

"I am angry that my last memories of Eric are ones of suffering, watching him in a hospital bed writhe with pain, hallucinate, put in restraints, wasting away to the point where he couldn't walk or bathe himself, or have a restful night. I am so thankful that I was able to spend some time with him during those dark moments, providing some comfort," Leeann went on to say, her voice brimming with pain.

"I will never understand, Ann, why you just didn't divorce him. Why did you have to torture him for months and make him endure such a painful death? He loved you and you completely and utterly betrayed him ultimately by taking his life. I will never forgive you and a lifetime in prison will never be enough time and enough punishment for what you've done to me and my family, but you will get your just punishment in death with eternity in hell," Leeann said full of rage.

At the end of the emotional hearing, Judge Stephens accepted the plea deal and sentenced Ann Miller to a minimum of twenty-five years and a maximum of thirty-one years and six months in prison. A small price to pay for a life, Morgan thought, but better than no price at all.

FINAL GOOD-BYE

"Naturally it wasn't the end of the story," Morgan says with his trademark grin, easing back into his chair.

Ann Miller had left Clare in the custody of her sister and brother-in-law Danielle and Dan Wilson, in Wilmington. (Paul Kontz hadn't been with the child long enough to really be a father to her.) Verus and Doris did not dispute the fact that the Wilsons loved Clare and took good care of her, but it bothered them tremendously that Clare was visiting her mother in prison. This was exactly what they did not want to happen. It had also come to their attention that when she spoke to her family, Ann was apparently in total denial of her guilt about the crime despite her guilty plea in court. She took no responsibility for Eric's death, and instead put all of the blame on Derril Willard.

Thus, in early 2006, when Ann Miller's murder trial would have begun had she not pleaded guilty, a custody dispute between Eric's family and Ann's family erupted. Verus and Doris, and Rich and Pam Baltzell, petitioned the court for joint custody of Clare. They accepted the fact that she would be in the physical custody of the Wilsons, but they wanted more time with her. They also asked New

Hanover County judge Phyllis Gorham to deny Ann any access to her daughter. Judge Gorham did grant the Millers joint custody of Clare, and in an even larger victory, she also granted an order preventing physical visits between Ann and Clare. This came after expert testimony from a doctor who interviewed Ann in prison and said she was still in total denial about her guilt. The judge kept the case open so that Danielle and Dan Wilson could petition the court at a later date to change this order when Clare was older and more able to understand the situation.

And there was also another unresolved issue. Against the Millers' wishes, Ann had had Eric's body cremated and interred at St. Francis of Assisi in Raleigh. For years Verus and Doris Miller had been fighting for custody of Eric's ashes so that they could bring him back to Indiana. It was all they had left of their son, and they desperately wanted him at home, where he belonged.

Morgan watched both of these battles from the sidelines. He had no power to help the Millers with issues in a civil courtroom; in fact, his mere presence might annoy the judge, given what a high-profile figure he'd been in the criminal case. So Morgan offered his emotional support. He met the Millers every time they came to Raleigh, be it for a meal, a chat, or simply a quick hug and an encouraging pat on the back.

When Ann pleaded guilty, the rights to Eric's ashes reverted to Ann's sister Danielle Wilson and her husband, as the executors of Clare's estate. As part of the custody arrangement, the Wilsons agreed to let the Millers take Eric's remains back to his hometown. While it appeared to be a symbolic gesture, to the Millers it was more, much more. It meant their boy was coming home. In July of 2006, the Millers had a proper funeral service for Eric, five and a half long years after his death. Morgan was honored to be invited, and he and Kay decided to make the six-hundred-mile trip. By car, of course.

"It was a time that I'll always remember," Morgan says wistfully.

While Morgan had gotten to know Eric over the years through the memories of his friends and family, it wasn't until he was in the house where Eric grew up, surrounded by his loved ones, that he really truly understood who Eric Miller had been. He was standing in the kitchen by the table where Eric had probably eaten a thousand breakfasts, blown out dozens of birthday candles, and spent countless hours doing his math homework. At once, all of the pieces came into place like a murky kaleidoscope image that suddenly comes into sharp focus. At that moment he knew that nothing he had done for Eric had been in vain. He realized that this all-American, squeaky-clean vision he had had of Eric over all these years had in fact been accurate.

But there was one more person who gave Morgan his final and clearest insight into Eric, one he carries with him to this day, and one that drove him to tell his story and share it with the world—Clare Miller. She was six years old by this time, not a baby, not yet a young lady, but a little girl trying to figure out who she was going to be. For Morgan, so much of the case had been about protecting Clare, but he realized that nothing he or anyone else could do would prevent the child from feeling the weight of her past, a past that she would never remember, but would surely learn about someday.

On July 24, 2007, the Millers went back to court after the Wilsons asked for Clare's visitation with Ann in prison to be reinstated. They also asked that "Wilson" be added to Clare's last name so that the child could be a "complete" member of their family. The Millers were strongly against both of these moves.

Danielle Wilson testified that Clare had become depressed and was acting out. She told the court that as her niece's de facto mother, the woman raising Clare, she should be able to decide what was right for Clare and, in Danielle's mind, seeing Ann might help the child.

"I am here because I see my child struggling, and I see her attitude affecting our house. I see her anger, and I see her sadness," Danielle said on the witness stand. "I love her dearly, and that is why this breaks my heart."

Danielle also testified that she had finally told Clare the truth about what her mother had done. Even with this information, she claimed that Clare still longed to visit Ann in prison.

" 'Ann was involved [in] and responsible for the death of Eric,' " Danielle Wilson testified, recalling her words to Clare at the dinner table one evening. " 'She is not here today because she is in prison. Ann stepped up and took responsibility. She said she was sorry. Dan and I have forgiven her.' "

Ultimately, a judge ruled that a trauma expert would be needed to decide whether or not Clare could see her mother, and also whether or not it was appropriate and necessary to add "Wilson" to Clare's last name.

But Morgan couldn't be concerned with what the court would do on these fronts. He was done. There was nothing more he could do. Yet he couldn't stop worrying about Clare. Seeing her in Indiana on the day of Eric's funeral—it was an image that he couldn't get out of his head.

"The child [Clare] appeared so frail and somewhat confused. There's almost a painful look to her [as if] somewhere deep down inside she understands on one level," Morgan says. "I still hope at some point and time she will understand everything."

But how could she understand? How could anyone ever truly understand Ann Miller's actions? These are questions Morgan still asks himself almost every day. He doesn't know where he will be when Clare Miller grows up, but he wants her to know the truth; not Ann's truth, but the real truth.

EPILOGUE

*There's a time for departure
even when there's no place to go.*
—TENNESSEE WILLIAMS

Morgan had a lot of time to think as he was driving home from Eric Miller's service, through the flatlands of Indiana, the rolling hills of Ohio, cutting across West Virginia into beautiful, green North Carolina.

"Why did Ann kill him?" Morgan remembers the question that kept kicking around in his head.

It was a question he has asked himself so many times over the years, yet he never came up with an answer, not even with miles of asphalt unrolling in front of him and nothing but landscape to ponder.

"Her [Ann's] love is a thin mask that hides a very monstrous creature on the inside, a creature that is totally self-consumed and self-involved, and that's not the way we were meant to live," Morgan concludes as he dissected Ann's personality one sharp country-road curve at a time.

It was on that lonely stretch of road from the Midwest to

the Southeast that the idea of sharing his story first came to Morgan like one of his many big ideas that never became reality. But this time, *this time* he would make it happen. He would share this story so that everyone, including Clare Miller, would know.

"I believe to this day that Ann Miller sleeps every night quite peacefully because I don't think she ever shed a righteous tear or spent a sleepless night worried about what she'd done to Eric," Morgan says scornfully.

Good homicide detectives know that *why* a crime is committed is something they may never fully discover, and they don't need to. What they need to know is who and how, period. Despite all of this wisdom, Morgan is a man who gave up on the *why*. And there's only one person who knows the answer he longed for—Ann Miller herself. Chances are it's a secret she's not planning on sharing with anyone, ever, especially not Chris Morgan.

"It's one of those mysteries that I'll never be able to fully grasp or understand," Morgan says regretfully. Yet even so, he now sleeps better than he has in years. Just knowing that Ann Miller is behind bars is enough for him.

As Morgan stands up from the old leather recliner, it's like a weight has suddenly lifted from his shoulders. He stretches and looks out the window as the rising sun peeks through the pine trees at the edge of his yard. He has a feeling of great relief and accomplishment. He did what he had set out to do. He finished the story. He finished it for himself, but most of all, he finished it for Clare.

Acknowledgments

I would like to thank my collaborators, especially Chris Morgan, for sharing his unbelievable story with me, and Dr. Michael Teague for sharing his expertise and insights. I would also like to thank the Raleigh Police Department and the Wake County District Attorney's Office for their professionalism and their assistance. I thank WRAL-TV for allowing me to cover this very fascinating story and giving me the resources to do it right.

I would like to thank the Millers for sharing Eric with me and most of all for giving me their blessings to write this book.

To my agent, Sharlene Martin—for your constant support and your tireless pursuit to make sure this story got published. To Shannon Jamieson Vazquez, my editor, for her hard work, patience, and understanding.

To my photographer, aka "work husband," Chad, thanks for the title and for putting up with me while I was writing and promoting two books. And to my real husband, Grif, my daughters, and my parents, thanks for always believing in me.

Amanda Lamb is a veteran television reporter for an award-winning CBS affiliate in the Southeast. She covers the crime beat for WRAL-TV. Her first book, *Smotherhood: Wickedly Funny Confessions from the Early Years* (Globe Pequot, August 2007) is a collection of nonfiction, humorous anecdotes about parenting. Amanda, her husband, and two daughters live in North Carolina. For more information about Amanda's writing go to www.DeadlyDoseBook.com.

Penguin Group (USA) Online

What will you be reading tomorrow?

Tom Clancy, Patricia Cornwell, W.E.B. Griffin,
Nora Roberts, William Gibson, Robin Cook,
Brian Jacques, Catherine Coulter, Stephen King,
Dean Koontz, Ken Follett, Clive Cussler,
Eric Jerome Dickey, John Sandford,
Terry McMillan, Sue Monk Kidd, Amy Tan,
John Berendt…

You'll find them all at
penguin.com

*Read excerpts and newsletters,
find tour schedules and reading group guides,
and enter contests.*

Subscribe to Penguin Group (USA) newsletters
and get an exclusive inside look
at exciting new titles and the authors you love
long before everyone else does.

PENGUIN GROUP (USA)
us.penguingroup.com

M224G1107